IRREFUTABLE
THE ORIGIN OF LIFE

HARRY J. (HERC) PALMQUIST

Irrefutable
by Harry J. Palmquist
Copyright ©2023, 2024 Harry J. Palmquist
ISBN 978-1-63360-226-7

All rights reserved under International Copyright Law. Written permission must be secured from the publisher/author to reproduce, copy, or transmit any part of this book.

Scripture quotations are taken from the NEW KING JAMES VERSION®. Copyright© 1982 by Thomas Nelson, Inc. Used by permission. All rights reserved.

For Worldwide Distribution Printed in the U.S.A.

Urban Press
P.O. Box 8881
Pittsburgh, PA 15221-0881 USA
412.646.2780
www.urbanpress.us

DEDICATION

This book is dedicated to those who bring me the greatest joy—my amazing family. The Lord has given me many talents, but the greatest thing God has given me is a wonderful family. So, I dedicate my book to my oldest daughter, Beckie; her husband, Phillip; and to her children and my grandchildren, JD, Dillon, Toby, and Braden. And to my son and sidekick, Jonny; and to my youngest daughter, Debbie (Cuddle Bug), and her husband, Trevar; and to her children, and my grandchildren, Bailee and Brody. And I cannot leave out my two big brothers, Fred and Ernie. God bless you all!

Table of Contents

Dedication
Acknowledgements
Introduction

chapter 1 Truth	1
chapter 2 Facts	5
chapter 3 Nothing	10
chapter 4 The Rock	14
chapter 5 Evolutionary Philosophy	18
chapter 6 Evolution Disqualified	22
chapter 7 Evolutionary Goals	27
chapter 8 It's Time	32
chapter 9 The Great Flood	36
chapter 10 Continents Divided	40
chapter 11 Dr. Stanley Miller and Darwin	44
chapter 12 Questions to Ask	48
chapter 13 Systems	52

chapter 14 DNA	56
chapter 15 Transitional Forms	61
chapter 16 Precision	64
chapter 17 Water	68
chapter 18 Fresh Water	73
chapter 19 Clean Air	76
chapter 20 Biosphere II	79
chapter 21 The Perfect Planet	83
chapter 22 The Creator	87
chapter 23 The Savior	91
chapter 24 Creation	97
chapter 25 Creation Continued	102
chapter 26 Creation Completed	106
Conclusion	90
Personal Note	93
Credits	94
About the Author	95

ACKNOWLEDGEMENTS

 Thank you to my Texas Christian School staff, some close friends, and even people I didn't know, who helped me with the content of this book. I want to thank Jim Rankin for his help in finding an appropriate cover that would reflect the awesome creativity of God.
 I would also like to thank Amanda Tarvin for taking the time to photograph the very special photo on the back cover – it is perfect! And a special thanks to Sara Cantu who initially helped me get my book started. And a very, very special thank you to Laurie Kendall who worked tirelessly on every aspect of this book. She pushed, pulled, typed, and retyped. There would be no book at this point if it wasn't for her "Can do" attitude, and her constant encouragement to stay on task and complete the mission at hand.

Introduction

The big question for all time is: "When and how did life begin?" That's a really good question. I thought most everyone when asked that question would respond, "Yeah, that's a good question." Or they would say, "We came from monkeys." But most of the people I interviewed for this book had never thought too much about life and its beginning. I was happy to bring these things to the forefront of their minds, even for a minute, and I appreciate their input to the content of this book. Almost all of those I interviewed liked the idea of having a part in the writing of a book. I didn't have any negative feedback at all. On the contrary, they showed great interest in talking about its content.

It's our desire that you, as a reader, will enjoy and be challenged by the content of this book as well: the simplicity of the message, the presentation of the facts, and the logical conclusions. But initially, when asked the question, "When and how did life begin?", most said, "I don't know." Some said, "You can't know." A few said, "It's a religious thing," and a few responded, "It just happened." As we went through the interview, I was able to share the facts that I am about to share with you. For most of them, it was an "ah ha" moment. They had learned something that was a life-changing experience, while for most, it was something new to think about.

I am one who really enjoys science. I have taught science for multiple grade levels over the years but the discipline I enjoy the most is biology: the study of life. It is fascinating how many life forms exist and each one has a purpose. There is a unique balance in nature such as the size and number of different animals. For instance, consider ants. Those industrious little critters sometimes cause major problems.

But, just think of what it would be like if ants were the size of sheep, and still had the numbers of the smaller version. Now there would be a problem. But fortunately that scenario will never happen because there is an unwritten law that keeps critters in check. Just think what it would be like if mosquitos were the size of birds. Again, this could never happen. Science never ceases to amaze me. Many, many books have been written about different animals and their features but few have addressed the question of how and when did life begin. Darwin never offered a suggestion in his book so I have chosen to answer the question myself. It's a fresh approach in understanding the study of life.

Most people respond to simple logic when asked logical questions. So I determined to find out if this was true or not. I made a list of twenty questions that I could ask without being too personal or intimidating. Basically I would just pick out people who were near to where I was at any time. For instance, I was at the lake with my family and I would talk with anyone who was just there relaxing, explaining that I was writing a book on the beginning of life. I don't believe I had anyone turn me down.

I was on a plane going to visit my brother and had an opportunity to talk to several people at the airport. I was bowling with my family and was able to talk to the people in the next lane. I was at McDonalds and was able to talk to a group of college students. I interviewed my doctors and nurses while I was under their care. I was part of a Parkinson's study and I interviewed the people involved in that.

I tried not to influence those I was interviewing one way or the other because I wanted their conclusion to be their own thoughts. If time permitted, I would go back over the questionnaire and answer any questions they might have. The reason that this is such an important question—"How and when did life begin?"—is because it reveals where one stands with God. And the purpose of this book is to provide a scientific approach to the answer of why you should believe in God.

The first topic we will be diving into will be the importance of truth. Truth is not just a word. It is a declaration of our commitment to continue to search for truth. Why is truth so important? Truth is important because it lays a foundation upon which to build one's character. If someone is known to be truthful or has a reputation for telling the truth, they have reached the pinnacle in their quest for excellence. Because, when all else fades away, truth will stand strong and tall, much like Superman who fights for "truth, justice, and the American way."

TRUTH

chapter 1

Truth

This book is devoted to the search and discovery of truth relating to the origin of life. Truth is truth and does not change with time or circumstances. It is the focal point of anything worth pursuing. Truth is like the wind in the sails of progress. It is like the Law of Gravity; it is consistent and absolute. There are those who might say things which were once thought to be true, but changed their mind when more information was discovered. For example, some once thought that the earth was flat but later discovered that the earth was round. And some thought at one time the earth was the center of the universe but later discovered that the planets revolve around the sun. Those original thoughts were not based on facts but rather incomplete or faulty information. When Sir Isaac Newton discovered gravity, he discovered it based upon facts. Truth is absolute and irrefutable.

> Truth is truth and does not change with time or circumstances.

Therefore, truth is a highly-prized commodity. Those who walk in truth are regarded as being special and unique. When Jesus stood before Pilate, Pilate asked Jesus, "What is truth?"

(John 18:38). Pilate had a unique opportunity to address the Creator of the universe. What an experience to tell his grandchildren about! Pilate was talking to Truth incarnate—Truth with skin on.

Throughout time, truth has been the ultimate characteristic of those who are held in high esteem. The reason that they are so respected is because their lives reflect the radiance of truth itself. Thomas Jefferson in his preamble to the constitution said, "We hold these truths to be self-evident." In other words, truth should be evident and easily recognized when being observed. And, as Ralph Waldo Emerson once said, "Truth is the property of no individual, but is the treasure of all men." Truth is something that should be desirable to enrich our lives; and we should endeavor to make truth a constant companion.

Here are some quotes from people who also shared a passion for the truth:

> "For though we love both the truth and our friends, piety requires us to honor the truth first." – Aristotle

> "If you want to have a healthy mind, you must feed your mind with truth. You must feed your mind not with junk or poison but with truth." – Rick Warren

> "We must condition our mind to accept truth and be open to the benefits of what truth has to offer." – Anonymous

> "Truth never penetrates an unwilling mind." – Jorge Luis Borges

Throughout this book you will be given the truth so you can make the right determination concerning the origin of life. Some of what I want to share with you may be new or different than what you have heard before, but I assure you that it is the truth. I want to encourage you to search for truth and you will discover the extent to which truth can affect your life. Next we will be discovering how facts can help lead us to the truth about events from the past.

Points to Ponder

1. Truth doesn't change no matter the conditions, circumstances, or considerations.
2. Truth offers freedom—freedom to search out truth and "to boldly go where no one has gone before." You have freedom to seek out answers you want from sources you can trust.
3. Truth lasts forever and will not age or depreciate. It's a good investment.

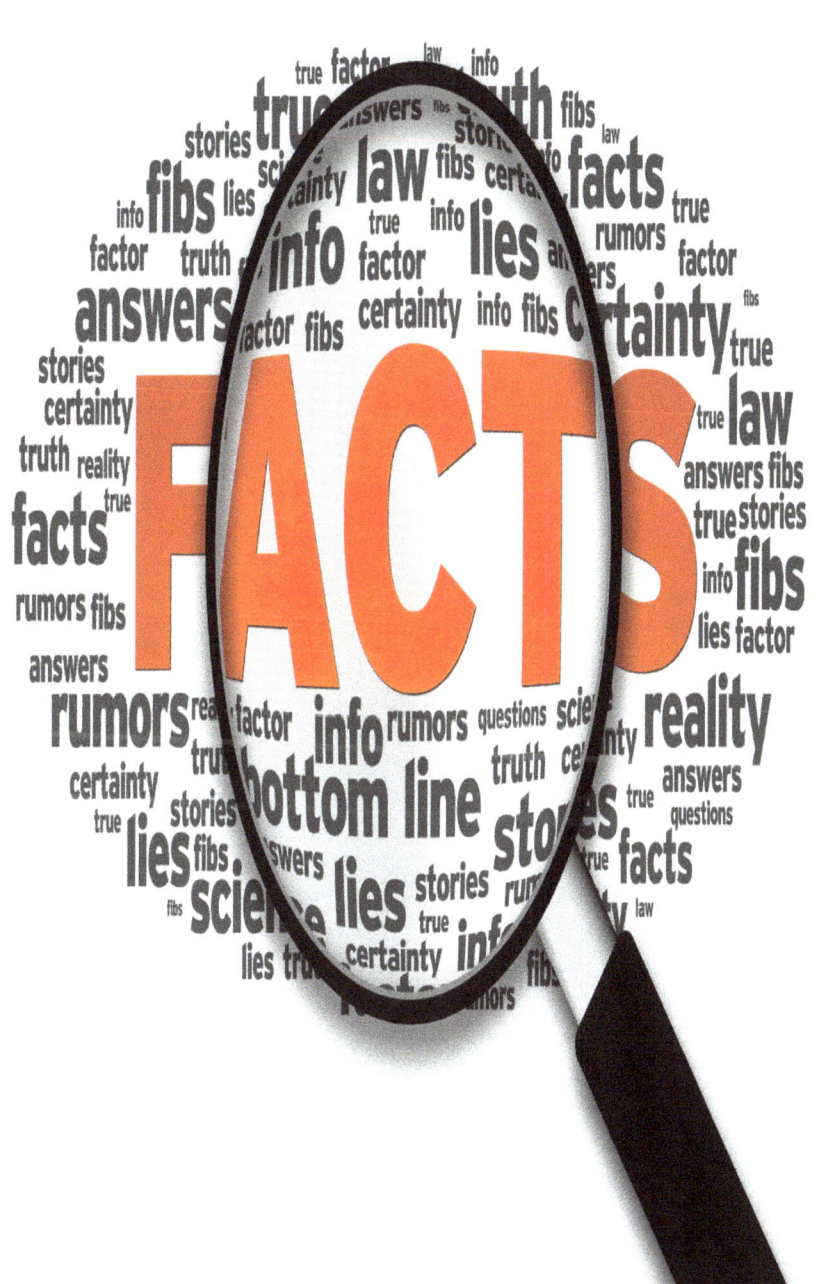

chapter 2

Facts

In this chapter, we will be talking about how truth is determined based on the facts and various methods of gathering information. Facts support the truth. They invite stats to check the validity of their presentation and they add security to life. The reader should be aware that facts can sometimes be misleading. There are some who will distort the facts in order to get the facts to agree with their particular philosophy or idea. They will use false information which will intentionally mislead so that one may reach a false conclusion. In this chapter, I have included an example of how facts can help determine the truth, as well as how facts can be used to mislead.

> Facts are facts. They care nothing what you think of them, neither will they change with your opinion.

As someone once said, "Facts are facts. They care nothing what you think of them, neither will they change with your opinion." This leads to the question: Is there truth that is absolute? The answer: Absolutely! If a truth changes, then it never was true to begin with, but merely an idea or philosophy not predicated on facts. Truth is not afraid of questions. On the contrary, truth reaches out with confidence to answer questions and never gets angry when challenged by another's opinion or point of view.

Years ago, I challenged some of my students in a science class to use their senses to determine what liquid was in each of ten jars using the scientific method which consists of:

1. Observe
2. Collect – Record data
3. Classify – Logical order, logical groups
4. Analyze – Determine the problem
5. Choose – Solution
6. Verify – Repeat experiment
7. Predict – What will happen in a similar situation

I had collected ten different clear liquids and put each of them into a separate glass jar. The following liquids collected were:

1. Water
2. Sprite
3. Hydrogen peroxide
4. Alcohol
5. Dish soap
6. Cooking oil
7. Karo Syrup
8. Clorox bleach
9. Camping fuel
10. Vinegar

The students had a list of the liquids so all they needed to do was label each jar with the substance they believed it to be. They could use all five senses to make that determination. Seldom did a student get all of them right. The fact that some of the liquids were labeled incorrectly by students did not change the contents of the jars. The substances remained the same regardless of whether the students determined the type of liquid correctly or incorrectly.

Facts can be generated through the scientific method because knowledge comes through observation. In fact, all our knowledge is gained through our five senses: what we see, what we hear, what we touch, what we smell, and what we taste. All the information that you receive comes into your mind through your senses and is stored in your brain for later use. This information also affects your preferences on what you like or dislike. This knowledge accumulates and is stored in automatically prepared compartments based on the priority of the moment.

Your brain is much like a sponge which can hold a lot of water. Unlike a sponge which can be saturated with water and overflow, the brain continues to function and absorb more input so that the more you learn the more you can learn! Information can stimulate the learning process and experiences can boost your attitude toward learning. The fact that you are reading this book indicates you desire more knowledge—and not just because you are reading it as a favor to me.

> **The more you learn, the more you can learn!**

In our next chapter we will be analyzing the facts concerning the origin of life on planet earth. And we will find that speculation is the key ingredient in the evolutionists attempt to find some cause to produce life without acknowledging the presence of God. In the next chapter will be looking at the topic of 'Nothing'—which affects everything.

Below are some quotes with facts for your consideration:

"The fact that a great many people believe something is no guarantee of its truth." - W. Somerset Maugham

"Facts do not cease to exist because they are ignored." - Aldous Huxley

As Sergeant Friday of an old television series would have said, "Just the facts, ma'am, just the facts!"

Points to Ponder

1. Facts establish the authenticity of the data that is being scrutinized.
2. Facts are specific as to what they are focused on.
3. Facts are worthy to be considered and accepted.

Nothing

chapter 3

Nothing

Let's continue our journey in the search for truth. The purpose of bringing up the topic of "Nothing" is to acknowledge the premise that there has always been something. That something is a "someone" who caused the physical universe to come into existence and has sustained it from the beginning.

> If at one time nothing existed, nothing would now exist.

Every journey must have a beginning, and *for there to be a beginning, there must be a cause.* A fire must have an ignition point. A design requires a designer. A building requires a builder. Information requires intelligence, and life requires a life-giver. In our search for truth, we will begin with this premise: "If at one time nothing existed, nothing would now exist." That is an absolute truth. Because things exists today, we must conclude that something has always existed.

Imagine if you can, as far back as you could go … into the far reaches of universe past. Imagine a time when there was only darkness and nothing else to stimulate activity. There was no light, no heat, and darkness filled all of space. It was a time when the temperature was near absolute zero and there was no movement of any kind. The silence was complete and life as we know it wasn't even a thought. Some would say that out of that nothingness there was a big bang or explosion and everything was set in motion to reach 2023 and beyond.

> Because things exist today, we must conclude that something has always existed.

Let's explore why the Big Bang Theory doesn't hold water. How do we know that? Well, for one, just watch the movie *Apollo 13*. When things began to malfunction and the astronauts had to shut down the computers, it didn't get hot inside the capsule—just the opposite—it got quite cold and ice formed on the equipment. The ground crew was concerned that the equipment wouldn't start up again. Even the sun didn't warm the capsule; which takes us back to the Big Bang bringing things into being.

Remember we said that for there to be a beginning, there must be a cause. If everything is near absolute zero—when there is no molecular movement and everything is at a standstill—there would be no cause to ignite a Big Bang explosion. There would be no energy to fire up the universe. Well, because things exist today, there has to be another reason for things to be here.

Also keep in mind our premise, "If at one time nothing existed, nothing would now exist." The universe had to come into existence through a supernatural means outside of a physical cause. Could it be that nothing was turned into something by the command of the Creator? Could it be that everything exploded into existence and the universe displayed the handiwork of an all-mighty Creator God? How can we know this is true?

> There would be no cause to ignite a big bang explosion.

Throughout this book I will give you examples of things that had to come into existence because of the design factor—the design of the universe by the Creator. Although the Creator is invisible to the human eye, He has left His fingerprints everywhere you look.

The next stop on our journey will be at Chapter 4: The Rock. Even though a rock is an inanimate, non-living object, it exists. And, because rocks are everywhere, could it be that they exist because they were created? We will cover how things began to form more in depth in our next chapter; and how ultimately you came to be in the 21st century. It will be a little harder—easier to read and understand—but harder to comprehend how much rocks have to say without saying a word. You will be amazed as we talk about rocks that talk!

Points to Ponder

1. Nothing means: not a thing.
2. Nothing is now something.
3. Nothing is incapable of doing anything.

ROCK

chapter 4

The Rock

Rocks speak without saying a word. If they could speak they would acknowledge their existence as proof that someone placed them here. We find that when considering how our universe began, we have two options, and only two. Our first option is that the universe would be an inanimate object void of any life. Our second option would be that there is a Creator capable of producing and sustaining life. Let's look at the implications of these two options.

> **The results of this experiment would be virtually no change.**

It's hard to comprehend the universe in its entirety, so let's consider a smaller inanimate object like a rock. Let's put that rock in an atmosphere conducive to life as we know it and provide it with organic food and water for a year. Over the course of a year, we will keep a log of any food and water offered to the rock and note any change in its size or shape.

Now, anyone making these observations would see that there would be no noticeable change in the rock. Say they were challenged to continue this exercise for another four years, for a total of five full years. During this time we would continue to offer food and water to the rock. We would bathe it, clothe it, and even sleep with it. We would keep up with the log and note any changes in the size or shape of the rock, or any characteristic that might be present in a typical lifeform. However, the results of this experiment would be virtually no change, regardless of the time period the rock was under observation.

You are probably thinking that this is absurd. Would anyone think that we just needed to give the rock more time? Let's assume someone could think that, so then for their benefit we would continue trying to create life out of a non-living object. Five years didn't give us the results we were looking for, so let's add a zero to the five. For 50 years, we would continue to feed and water the rock, noting any changes to it. However, knowing what we know about geology and biology, we can logically conclude that 50 years is not enough time to develop any kind of life in an inanimate object.

So, just to be sure we're observing our rock long enough, let's just add another "0" and extend our routine for a total of 500 years. Still no change would be evident. Let's just continue our experiment for 50,000 or 500,000 years and just suppose we continued our experiment for 500,000,000 years and so on. After all, what is one more zero in the realm of time?

No matter how many zeros would be added, the rock would not change or develop in any way; there would continue to be no signs of life. No matter how many years a rock exists, a rock will never grow or reproduce because a rock is an inanimate object and cannot support or exhibit any signs of life.

> No matter how many years a rock exists, a rock will never grow or reproduce.

On a much larger scale, the universe is an inanimate object with the same limitations as a rock. There are some who believe life could have begun in a pool of water ladened with just the right amount of minerals in a conducive environment that could produce all the ingredients necessary for life. That is a far-fetched theory that, as we have just seen, cannot be based in fact and therefore is not true.

In the next chapter, we will discuss evolutionary philosophy. We will find that "evolution is like a magician pulling a rabbit out of a hat? It's impressive, but it's a trick and not reality." The included quotes come directly out of a book on evolution which we will be taking about in our next chapter.

Points to Ponder

1. Rocks are a small part of a huge universe.
2. Rocks cannot speak but their presence on earth or on a table in a room says that they must have been there because someone placed them there.
3. Rocks cannot come to life because they are inanimate and lifeless objects.

chapter 5

Evolutionary Philosophy

A philosophy is how you think; and how you think is reflected in your actions. You really can't do anything without thinking about it; and when you think, you think in words. Again, evolution is like a magician pulling a rabbit out of a hat. It's impressive but it's a trick.

The Bible says in Colossians 2:8, "Beware lest any man spoil you through philosophy and vain deceit, after the traditions of men, after the rudiments of the world and not after Christ." In order not to buy into the evolutionary philosophy, it is best to fill your mind with truth found in the Bible. Romans 12:2 says, "And be not conformed to this world; but be transformed by the renewing of your mind, that you may prove what is that good and acceptable and perfect will of God."

A purpose of this book is to share the truth with those who don't know what the truth is; and hopefully, they will recognize the truth and respond to it. They should begin to think differently. And by thinking differently, they will acknowledge the flaws of evolution and reject them so that they can accept the truth of creation.

Evolutionists use the big numbers of millions and billions because it gives them a way to change directions if they come across any resistance to their claims. Right off the bat, they declare, *"Our planet and the rest of the solar system are now reckoned to be about 4.5 billion years of age: for most of that incomprehensibly long time the earth was lifeless."* *

The author continues, *"If life began as a molecule with the miraculous capacity to reproduce itself, developing later as a single cell and then into a cluster of a few soft cells, it could not possibly leave even the shadowiest imprint behind."**

"Yet somewhere on earth, somehow life indeed began, possibly more than two billion years ago."*

In the fullness of time, mutations and selection again performed their wonders."*

"There were new and better eggs. These eggs were internally fertilized and then deposited in some safe place until the young were hatched."*

The fish were evolving rapidly and growing into amphibians which were quickly evolving into reptiles. Understand, quickly means over millions of years. Then, of course would come birds and mammals after millions and millions more years. And here we are in the 21st century and evolutionists still believe that things are still evolving. The evolutionists look to the fossils to aid in their efforts to find something new and different to make evolution more believable. Something new and different

> Evolutionists cannot acknowledge that there was a flood.

from the fossils would be understanding the reality that the fossils are the result of the Great Flood of Noah. Fossils are formed when the living organisms are covered quickly with mud. This happened all over the world. The great layers of mud are seen in the walls of the Grand Canyon.

Of course, the evolutionists cannot acknowledge that there was a flood, because that would mean the Bible is true in that there really was a Great Flood. The results of the flood are obvious but they couldn't believe that because that would mean they would have to acknowledge God; and that would mean they would have to rethink their philosophy.

Evolution came on the scene and tried to steal the show. But evolution is like a snake—it doesn't have a leg to stand on.

They don't have any facts to bring to the table. That is why evolution has been disqualified which we will be discussing in the next chapter.

Points to Ponder

1. Evolutionary philosophy—there is no God.
2. Man is the ultimate authority.
3. Their goal is for you to trust in science—faulty science that is.

chapter 6

Evolution Disqualified

Evolution is disqualified because it is so aggressive that they overlook the truth that is so evident. Now that you have finished reading the previous chapter, let's go back and take a second look at what was said. But first, let's bring the evolutionary dates together into one clear compilation.

4.5 billion years ago – that's how old the earth is

3.6 billion years ago – there is no trace of fossils

2 billion years ago – the first traces of life

425 million years ago – a new fish was discovered

390 million years ago – new and different fish were found

365 million years ago – some fish ventured out on land

The dates and fish are unbelievable! Talk about pulling a rabbit out of a hat! There are no scales, no caliper, no yardstick—there are no means of measuring time—especially in billions of years or even millions of years. There are some dating methods for hundreds of years and thousands of years but even they are unreliable and not very accurate. There is no way to calculate what things were like millions and billions of years ago. It is totally hypothetical and yes, evolutionists throw out numbers as if they were feeding oats to a flock of chickens.

> Who is there to challenge their accuracy?

They just do it because they can, and who is there to challenge their accuracy or hold them accountable for what they say or put in writing? It is just assumed that the evolutionary dates are correct. And keep in mind, evolution has never been observed. Some say, "It's so slow, no one can see it!" While others say, "It goes so fast, no one can see it!" But either way, this is an example of evolution in action.

The second thing to note is that all life evolved around water. First there were single-celled animals, and then clusters of cells like jelly fish. Then there were water-dwelling invertebrates, and then vertebrates and fish. After that, there were fish that "decided" to live on land. Following them were lizards, monkeys, apes, and finally man. It is a wondrous thing to think that somewhere in our family tree there was a jelly fish. Again, there is no proof that one species ever turned into another species.

> There is no proof that one species ever turned into another species.

The third thing we need to note is the progress of how things moved to better themselves. They claim that mutations and selection were responsible for better fins and better swimming. Because of summer droughts, some fish ventured on land. To be able to take advantage of a new source of food, some fish developed a fish tail with lungs and well-developed legs and feet.

During 50 million to 100 million years, the fish spread far and evolved into many different species. Some amphibians (which can live in or out of water) developed its eggs to go from soft and unprotected to better eggs with a leathery shell; and somewhere along the line came reptiles. Birds and mammals went their separate ways. In all of this movement, why aren't we considering the existence of DNA? Who was programming who?

According to one book on evolution, the reproduction of a cell results in an exact replica of the original cell. This is true but when did the differences take place? Their answer to this is in their concept of mutations. The problem is that most mutations are harmful not beneficial. Mutations can affect the whole body or may not be noticeable at all. But many times the mutation will cause extra appendages to grow like an extra arm or leg—or even a head.

When I was young, we had a calf that was born with one complete body but it had two heads. It lived and grew for about six weeks until its heart gave out and it died. At other times, mutations may delete arms or legs, or even place the affected body part in an awkward place where hopefully it can be corrected through surgery.

> Most mutations are harmful, not beneficial.

In another book on evolution, it said that all the matter in the universe was at one time packed together in a dot as big as the period at the end of this sentence. Because everything was so packed, the friction within that little dot caused it to explode and become the universe as we know it. We are not talking about our solar system or our galaxy, but the universe. The problem with that theory is that everything we know about matter and the physical makeup of the universe indicates it's an impossibility because all the atoms in the universe could not be crammed into a dot.

This leads to the conclusion that evolution is not scientific at all, but a theory—and a poorly supported one at that. According to *Webster's Collegiate Dictionary*, evolution would not be classified as a theory but maybe just a hypothesis. And the word "theory" is defined as, "The analysis of a set of facts in their relation to one another." There are no facts in evolution and it could be and probably is, just a philosophy—a way of thinking.

Evolutionists don't have the facts and therefore they use their imaginations so they can sound authoritative on the matter, presenting theory as scientific fact. Evolution is disqualified because its proponents overlook the truth that is so evident. They continue to say the species can produce different species. If they had their way, they would eliminate anything having to do with God or the Bible altogether, which we will discuss in greater detail in the next chapter.

POINTS TO PONDER

1. Evolution is not a scientific entity but merely a philosophy.
2. Evolution doesn't have any facts to support its claims.
3. Evolution doesn't have any beneficial attributes.

chapter 7

Evolutionary Goals

Evolutionists have very aggressive goals. If they could, they would eliminate the Bible, churches, and anything else religious. They would dominate school text books, magazines, TV programming, movies, and anything else that goes against their philosophy. They do what they can to influence those who will listen.

> Evolutionists will do everything they can because they can.

As I have said before, they will do everything they can because they can. They aren't held accountable for what they say or put in writing. For the most part, whatever they have to say is accepted without being challenged. Hopefully, this book's scientific presentation of truth will cause people to consider what we have to say.

The study of life is the strength of our position and presentation. The Bible says, "In Him (Jesus) was life; and the life was the light of men" (John 1:4). Light and truth are synonymous in the Bible. The above verse says that when we look at living things, it is obvious that there is a Creator. Life has to have a life-giver. In the first chapter of the book of Romans, verse 20 says, "For the invisible things of Him from the creation of the world, are clearly seen, being understood by the things that are made, even His eternal power and Godhead, so that they are without excuse."

This verse is telling us that the invisible things of God are clearly seen—although we are made from atoms and molecules, we can still see that we are created with active ingredients. We can clearly see and understand that God created us through His power and Godhead creativity. It is so clear, so rational and logical, that those who deny the creation are without excuse. In other words, those who don't believe cannot say, "I didn't know!" There is no excuse because it is so obvious.

Hebrews 11:3 says: "Through faith we understand that the worlds were framed by the word of God, so that things which are seen were not made of things which do appear." Here is another reference to being made of atoms and molecules—things that we cannot see. Evolutionists are what the Bible calls "willingly ignorant" of the heavens and the earth (2 Peter 3:5).

> These people are willingly ignorant so they are without excuse.

A good description of evolutionists is found in 2 Timothy 3:7 where it says, "They were ever learning, and never able to come to the knowledge of the truth." These evolutionary leaders were constantly learning how to deceive and sound like they had truth, while in reality never coming close to it. These Scriptures hit the nail on the head.

There is an abundance of evidence that points to a creator. It is sad it think that there are intelligent people who listen to the evolutionary propaganda and choose not to believe the truth of a creator. As the Scripture says, These people are willingly ignorant so they are without excuse. They cannot say, "I didn't know." As we have said, "Truth is evident!"

How many times have you heard it said, "This or that happened over a million years ago?" There is no truth in that. There is no way they can calculate that amount of time and be accurate. So the next time you hear it said, "That happened millions of years ago!" ask, "How do you know"?

Another evolutionary goal is their agenda to reduce the

world's population, as well as genetic engineering. This is all a part of the evolutionary philosophy:

"The time is not far off when man will have to regulate his numbers, and control his genetic patrimony in order to sustain his body and mental vigor. Knowledge and understanding are the prime requisites for a successful response to the great challenge, which is really a challenge to survival. To help people to acquire such knowledge and understanding is the aim of the book."*

Did you catch that in the first of this paragraph? "The time is not far off when man will have to regulate his numbers …" We're not only talking about birth control, but we're also talking about an agenda to reduce the world's population. Their goal is to challenge biblical thinking and replace it with evolutionary thinking.

> Their goal is to challenge biblical thinking and replace it with evolutionary thinking.

Once again, time and accountability are the keys that unlock the evolutionary doors. Evolutionists believe time is on their side. King David in Psalms 90:12 says, "So teach us to number our days, that we may apply our hearts unto wisdom." He prayed that God would teach us to number our days because time is limited. In this life, you may have 70, 80, or even 90 years, but that is about it.

> We were created to believe in God.

As believers in God, we should not put humans in the mammalian box because humans are more than just mammals. Humans were created in the image of God. We were created to be like God: to think, reason, care, plan, create, and enjoy life and all it has to offer. There are those who would say they are atheists but they were not born that way. Someone along the line influenced their thinking. We were all born believing that there is a God. Ask almost any little child if there is a God and their response will be "sure."

When new families enroll in the school where I teach, we would have family meetings with them to go over some of the things in my book. I would intentionally pick out one of the four or five year olds, and we would discuss the "rock." I would ask, "Can a rock grow or develop eyes? Can a rock eat your snack? Can a rock swim in the aquarium with fish?"

Of course, the answers are all "no" and children knew that. They knew an inanimate object, whether it is a rock or a universe, cannot see or eat anything—it really cannot do anything. And even though rocks cannot do anything, they still shout out that there is a God. How do we know? Because they are here. They could not produce or reproduce themselves. Someone had to place them here.

> We were all born believing there is a God.

In our next chapter, we will be discussing time. Time is limited and you only get one shot at it so we must make it count. It's important for us to leave a legacy behind us. As someone once said, "Time is of the essence." Time and life make a great combination—handle them with care.

Points to Ponder

1. Evolutionists want people to reject biblical thinking and replace it with evolutionary thinking.
2. Another evolutionary goal is their agenda to reduce the world's population, as well as genetic engineering.
3. Evolutionists are what the Bible calls "willingly ignorant" of the heavens and the earth (see 2 Peter 3:5).

chapter 8

It's Time

Earlier I mentioned the asexual reproduction of cells when a single cell reproduces by splitting in half. The important thing to remember is that the single-celled offspring is always identical with the parent. If that is so (and it is), then the variations of the cell would be quite limited. Sexual reproduction is different because you have two parents involved.

The one thing that evolution's proponents do is pull numbers out of ages past and use them to justify their belief that time is the creator, not God. For instance, some claim our solar system is 4.5 billion years old. How do they come up with that number? No one has ever seen evolution take place, so how can they possibly prescribe a date or time without knowing how to calculate the right outcome?

> Evolution believes our solar system is 4.5 billion years old.

The same would go for the 3.6 billion years to attribute to the beginning of life. They say that *somewhere* on earth, *somehow* life began, possibly more than two billion years ago. They are still pulling rabbits out of a hat! They continue to say what happened when rocks formed about 425 million years ago.

"The reason for all the time was because it took some doing by the infant sciences of geology and archeology, to give this evolutionary concept enough time to operate in—a few thousands of millions of years instead of a few thousand years."* Still they pull the rabbit out of the hat. So, to put it all together, here is the synopsis.

> They say that somewhere on earth, somehow life began.

There are those who don't believe in a Creator God. And rather than seek out God, they choose to put their time and energy into finding someone or something else other than God. That something is evolution. That someone is anyone who believes in evolution and not God. So, the first thing on their intellectual agenda is to eliminate God and find an explanation for the beginning of life without God. Their efforts are wrapped up in time—time is their friend. If you need more time, no problem—just add more zeroes.

> Time is their friend.

The second thing on the agenda is to create a diversion or distraction, anything that can make believers look foolish or insecure in their faith, such as: "Don't tell me you believe in Noah's ark! How does he get all those animals on that little itty bitty boat? Oh, and how about that guy, Jonah, who got swallowed by a big fish?" The third thing on the agenda is to recruit more unbelievers, especially those who are in important positions in their fields of education.

The fourth thing on the agenda is to produce books, textbooks, TV documentaries, or movies with an evolutionary premise and fill them with evolutionary concepts. If they are not sure of something, they proceed like it's true, even if it's not. Their goal is to make evolution the accepted way of thinking and as natural as breathing. The fifth thing on the agenda is

> They write books, textbooks, TV programs, movies or magazines to make evolution the accepted way of thinking.

> Evolution claims life began in a pool of water.

to attack anyone who doesn't believe in the evolutionary philosophy, and make them out be the simpletons who want to ruin lives and lead people astray.

"The world came into being about 4.5 billion years ago. Given enough time, life began in a pool of water with all the ingredients necessary for life. Life was simple, and the first cells prospered. After a period of time, these single cells began to cluster and form multi-cellular organisms. The cluster then grew to become a jellyfish."*

"Time went on and more clusters of cells turned into fish. The oceans began to teem with life. Some of the ocean creatures ended up crawling up on land and became the first amphibians. These animals went back and forth from the water. Some that stayed on land developed forearms and legs to get around better. These became the first reptiles. Because most of the living creatures still lived in the water, those creatures that stayed on land flourished because of the abundance of food and the reptiles ruled the land and literally took over the earth."*

> Evolution claims after a period of time, these single cells began to cluster.

Because of the wickedness and violence of men, God told Noah to build an ark because God was going to cover the earth with a great flood. In our next chapter, we will be discussing the discovery of fossils and also how there are many stories that have been passed down through time from various cultures about a great flood.

POINTS TO PONDER

1. Evolutionists believe that time is the creator—not God.
2. No one has ever seen evolution take place.
3. The goal of evolutionists is to make their theory the accepted way of thinking.

chapter 9

The Great Flood

We have not spent much time on fossils but they are important in the realm of creation. Fossils are an imprint in the rocks that were once mud. How is mud created? The fossils were buried when water soaked the ground and they were quickly covered by mud. They were encased in the mud and embedded until something or someone unearthed them. But why do we sometimes find fossils on top of mountains? Good question. The answer is: There was once water that high.

> There are over 100 stories of a great flood.

Maybe you don't believe that but the evidence is there. There are over 100 stories in various cultures of a great flood that covered the earth to the tops of mountains, with variations of the stories explaining that a few people were saved from the flood by being in a boat. In this great flood, many people, animals, plants, and trees were buried under the mud from the great flood. One of those stories comes from the Bible and is very detailed.

As the story goes, God told Noah to build a big boat (they called it an ark) and put lots of different animals on it along with his family, because God was going to flood the earth due to the fact that the people were quite corrupt and extremely violent. So Noah built the ark and got the animals and his family onboard before the flood came.

The Bible says that it rained for 40 days and 40 nights until the hills and mountains were covered by water, approximately 22 feet above the highest mountain. That is how and why we find fossils on the mountains all over the world from top to bottom.

> The fossils tell us that the animals were fully developed.

What the fossils tell us is that the animals were fully developed, showing no evidence of transitional forms of life. How do we know that the flood was worldwide? Because there are fossils all over the world and the rock strata is in layers like we see when we visit the Grand Canyon. However, you may wonder how the Grand Canyon was created and carved out of the earth to such a magnitude? Let me explain.

After the water of the flood decreased and dry land appeared, Noah and his family left the ark. The earth was at this time still one huge continent called Pangia and remained that way for about 325 years. During that time period, Noah and his family had traveled a long way from the ark. The topography of the land varied greatly and two lakes formed north of what would become the Grand Canyon.

> The once great land mass became seven different continents

The Bible says that one of Noah's grandsons, Eber, had two sons, and one of them was named Peleg. The name Peleg means divided, like splitting an apple. Genesis 10:25 says, "For in his days, was the earth divided". Eber named his son Peleg because this splitting or divide was an important event and one to be remembered. The huge land mass divided, broke apart, and the once great land mass became the seven different continents which we will be discussing more in depth in our next chapter.

POINTS TO PONDER

1. In Texas we say, "Remember the Alamo." In Noah's day, we would have said, "Remember the Flood."
2. There are over 100 stories in different cultures that tell the stories of a number of people saved from a great flood by being on a boat.
3. Noah and his family and all the animals got off the ark somewhere near Mount Ararat in what today is the country of Turkey.

chapter 10
Continents Divided

Now, let's get back to the Grand Canyon. When this division took place, the two lakes in the north split and the water rushed south, tearing out a huge section of land. What remained is known as the Grand Canyon. Look at a picture of the Canyon and you will notice the multi-layering of the strata which was a result of the Flood.

It is said that the Colorado River carved out the Grand Canyon over millions of years. When we look at Mount St. Helen's volcanic eruption, the lake that was on the mountain broke out and carved out a canyon very similar to what happened with the Grand Canyon. It only took eight hours to carve out a canyon like the Grand Canyon. That is common knowledge. So, in Peleg's day, when the two lakes broke out, it required only a matter of a few days to carve out the Grand Canyon—such is the power of raging water.

> Such is the power of raging water.

From what would become Africa, to what would become the Americas—which became the Western Hemisphere—the continents as we know them today came into being. And as the land pulled away, moved and buckled, the Rocky Mountains were formed on the west coast of Canada and the United States and continued down through Central America and extending all the way to Chili and Argentina in South America. Other mountains formed on the east coast but they were not as big as those on the west coast. They are called the Smokey Mountains. You can actually see the di-angled rocks as you travel in those mountains.

The continents are now pretty stationary but occasionally there will be earthquakes and volcanic eruptions. Both people and animals moved along with the land masses. So, if you have ever wondered how people and animals arrived at different locations around the world, it happened during the days of Peleg. That's another reason why different animals are unique to different parts of the world. Here is a breakdown of where different animals are found:

> If you have ever wondered how people arrived at different locations around the world ...

It sure makes a big difference to think of the land shifting as compared to people crossing a land bridge across the Arctic and going all the way to South America. The shift is explained in the Bible; and if you have questions, the Bible has the answers—that is ... if you are interested in the facts.

In the next chapter, we will be covering an experiment performed by a man by the name of Dr. Stanley Miller, who

Australia	Koala Bears, kangaroos, platypus, the Tazmanian Devil and more
Africa	Elephants, lions, hippos, cheetahs, leopards and many more
Euroasia	Indian elephant, tiger, mongoose, camel, snow leopard, panda
South America	Kamen, taper, sloth, jaguar, anteater, llama
North America	Bison, pronghorn antelope, cougar

sought to create life in his science lab using some common elements. Please keep in mind that a follow-up experiment to his was never conducted.

POINTS TO PONDER

1. In Peleg's day, the earth was divided—split like an apple—and formed the seven continents.
2. During the shift the land buckled, and the mountains were formed on the west coast as the Americas and Canada pulled away from Africa.
3. When the earth divided into continents, both men and animals were relocated to other parts of the world.

chapter II

Dr. Stanley Miller and Darwin

In 1953, Professor Stanley Miller at the University of Chicago conducted an experiment combining hydrogen, methane, ammonia, and water vapor. He zapped the concoction with an electric current— simulating lightning—and waited for the results. After five days, Miller discovered what he had hoped for—a few simple amino acids—which are the basic building blocks of a living organism. Miller felt his experiment laid the groundwork to prove that these essential components of life could have formed somewhere in the vast pools of water somewhere on the earth.

It must be noted that Miller's experiment was conducted under carefully planned controls and by manipulating the conditions. All the elements of the experiment were specifically designed procedures for performing the experiment under the watchful eye of an intelligent being.

Miller theorized that if one showed scientifically that life could form without any outside assistance but could emerge from naturalistic causes, it would add credibility to the theory of evolution. It would mean that life could evolve through undirected processes completely devoid of a purpose or plan. But what was not revealed about Miller's experiment was that the amino acids which were formed were not living; they were merely a concoction of lifeless chemicals resting in the waters of an experimental test lab.

Dr. Miller performed his experiment before DNA was discovered. When he found the amino acids he made, there was no way he could have developed an organism because DNA is responsible for the development of all lifeforms. DNA is programmed to build an organism and the program is developed and produced by God. At this point in time, we do not have the technology to program DNA. We can work with bits and pieces of it, but that's all we can do. It's interesting that no one has ever picked up on his findings and tried to replicate the experiment.

> The amino acids which were formed were merely a concoction of lifeless chemicals resting in the waters of an experimental test lab.

Now let's consider if life did or can form through this type of spontaneous generation. Darwin believed that cells were the beginning of life and were simple organisms with a makeup much like that of gelatin. He believed that these early lifeforms would not only survive but would prosper in the early environment of creation. That's quite an intellectual stretch and one that requires a lot of faith — more faith perhaps than believing in the existence of an intelligent Creator who was behind the beginning of the world.

> The experiment had specifically designed procedures.

Darwin had no idea how complex cells could be. Every cell has all nine systems functioning in it. Neither did Darwin know anything about DNA. Perhaps if Darwin knew as much as we know today, he never would have suggested the idea of evolution. And he would not be responsible for many people rejecting

> Darwin believed that cells were the beginning of life – they were simple organisms with a makeup much like gelatin.

God. As it is, Darwin took the facts that we have discovered and distorted them with false ideas of evolution and rejected the truth of creation and the facts that supported it.

    Questions keep your mind active and wanting to know more. Socrates taught mostly from questions. A lot of your questions will be answered in the next chapter called Questions to Ask.

POINTS TO PONDER

1. The results of the experiment were predictable.
2. The experiment was carefully planned and executed.
3. The experiment was successful in producing simple amino acids but did not produce life.

chapter 12

Questions to Ask

The question to consider if these cells formed as Darwin suggested is, "What did they eat?" In order for these cells to continue to live, they would have to consume something of nutritional value. Whatever it was, it had to be organic. One could certainly satisfy appetite cravings by eating sand, but there would not be any nutritional value.

The second question that one might ask is, "How did it eat?" Cells do not have mouths, but have tiny little holes in the cell membrane. Through these holes, the cell must determine what has nutritional value and what does not. As a result, the cell is able to consume the right kind of food necessary to keep the cell alive.

Once the cell is able to ingest food, a third question would need to be asked: "How would the cell digest and distribute the nutrients throughout the cell to give it the energy it needs to thrive?" Then a fourth question would arise: "How would the cell eliminate the toxins and waste products produced by the digestive process?"

All these necessities would have to have immediate answers otherwise there would be no way for these life functions to develop over a period of time. Finally, the cell would have to be able to breathe, move, and respond to stimuli, such as light, heat, and cold—as well as be able to reproduce. All these life functions or systems would have to be functioning at the same time in order for the cell to survive.

As we continue to advance forward, we are about half way through this book. Hopefully by this time, you have generated enough interest that you have a bug inside of you that wants to know more. Perhaps you are thinking, "How can these things be?"

Remember, I said from the beginning that this book is grounded in truth. If you don't believe what I'm saying, then prove it wrong. Remember, truth is not afraid of questions. Perhaps you have read or heard things that are contrary to what is written here. Remember that bug we spoke of earlier that wants to know more?

> Questions to ask:
> 1. What did they eat?
> 2. How did they eat?
> 3. How would the cell digest and distribute the nutrients?
> 4. How would the cell eliminate the toxins and waste products?
> 5. When would the cell take its first breath?
> 6. When would the cell feel the need to move, respond to stimuli, and know the purpose of reproduction?

When my children were young, the occasional visit to Wal-Mart would lead to the inevitable words, "I want that!" We, as good parents would say "No, your want bug is going to eat you." Well, that same bug lives inside of you and it wants to know as much as you can feed it about who, what, where, when, why and how. You must feed this bug in order to keep your interest in learning and growing. You see, questions are a good instructional mechanism that provokes interest and helps us gain knowledge.

> There is a bug that lives inside of you that needs to know about who, why, where, when, and how.

Socrates was a master teacher and philosopher in Greece, especially when it came to the art of asking good questions. He believed that a seasoned teacher is one who knows how to lead instruction by asking good, as well as, the right questions.

In the next chapter we will delve into the nine systems which every organism or body has in greater detail. All nine of these systems keep our bodies running smoothly and are essential for life to exist, to the extent that if just one of the nine malfunctioned or was removed, the whole body or the organism would begin to die.

POINTS TO PONDER

1. Questions are a good thing to help focus on the objective.
2. Questions often lead to more questions.
3. Questions often lead to a different conclusion.

chapter 13

Systems

Every lifeform is uniquely created and has systems specifically designed to support its life's purpose. We have nine systems in all that keep our bodies, as well as every other organism, running smoothly.

The *skeletal system* provides the organisms structure either for the internal function like with mammals, birds, fish, reptiles and amphibians, or the exoskeleton such as what we find in bugs. The *muscular system* makes it possible for the organism to move in one direction or another.

The *digestive system* enables the organism to acquire the necessary nutrients to get the energy it needs to survive. The *respiratory system* enables the organism to inhale the oxygen it needs, and exhale the carbon dioxide, waste products, and toxins produced by the operation of the respiratory system.

The *circulatory system* aids in the delivery of oxygen and nutrients throughout the body, as well as tends to the removal of carbon dioxide, waste products, and toxins produced by the everyday functioning of the body. The *urinary system* acts as a filter for the blood by removing various waste products and flushing them from the body. The *endocrine system* has glands which control bodily functions by producing hormones. These chemicals are released into the blood which then carries them throughout the body.

The *nervous system* functions like a conductor of a multi-instrument orchestra. It directs and coordinates all the activities of the other systems and enables them to respond and adjust to changes that occur within itself and its surroundings.

The *reproductive* system. First of all, it is asexual, as each cell membrane divides in half without any breaking or tearing of the cell membrane. At the same time, sexual reproduction occurs with all multicellular organisms—humans, mammals, birds, reptiles, and amphibians.

> **The Systems and Their Purpose**
> 1. Skeletal System
> 2. Muscular System
> 3. Digestive System
> 4. Respiratory System
> 5. Circulatory System
> 6. Urinary System
> 7. Endocrine System
> 8. Nervous System
> 9. Reproduction System
>
> All the systems support one another and work together as one unit.

All of the above systems support life. They work together for the health and well-being of the organism. Each system was specifically designed to handle the needs of the organism and support the purpose of the other systems. Each system is unique and indispensable to the overall health of the whole body.

For instance, the skeletal system gives support to the body enabling it to move without collapsing; and at the same time, the backbone encases the nervous system—spinal cord—protecting it from injury. All body functions are controlled by the brain which is connected to the different organs by the spinal cord. A chiropractor will tell you that an "adjustment" is necessary so there is clear communication between each organ and the brain.

> **Each system is indispensable**

These systems are extremely important to life because if one malfunctions, the rest of the organs suffer as well.

For example, if the respiratory system is struggling, the other systems won't get the oxygen they need and will begin to shut down. The muscular system will begin to weaken, the circulatory system slows down as not enough oxygen is being circulated throughout the organism, etc.

Each system is indispensable in that if one system fails, the organism will begin to die. In order for the organism to live and thrive, all systems have to be operational from the beginning. There is no time for the systems to develop. You can't postpone breathing for a while, or you won't be breathing at all. You can't live without the nervous system because no organism can function without its brain. All the systems are necessary for life, throughout the lifecycle of the organism.

> All the systems are necessary for life.

In the next chapter, we are going to discuss DNA. DNA is the programmed instruction manual for how an organism is going to function. Every living thing is the result of the instructions it has been given by God. We will be discovering how DNA has God's fingerprints all over it.

POINTS TO PONDER

1. Systems are necessary to function in life.
2. Systems care for specific needs.
3. Systems all work 24/7.

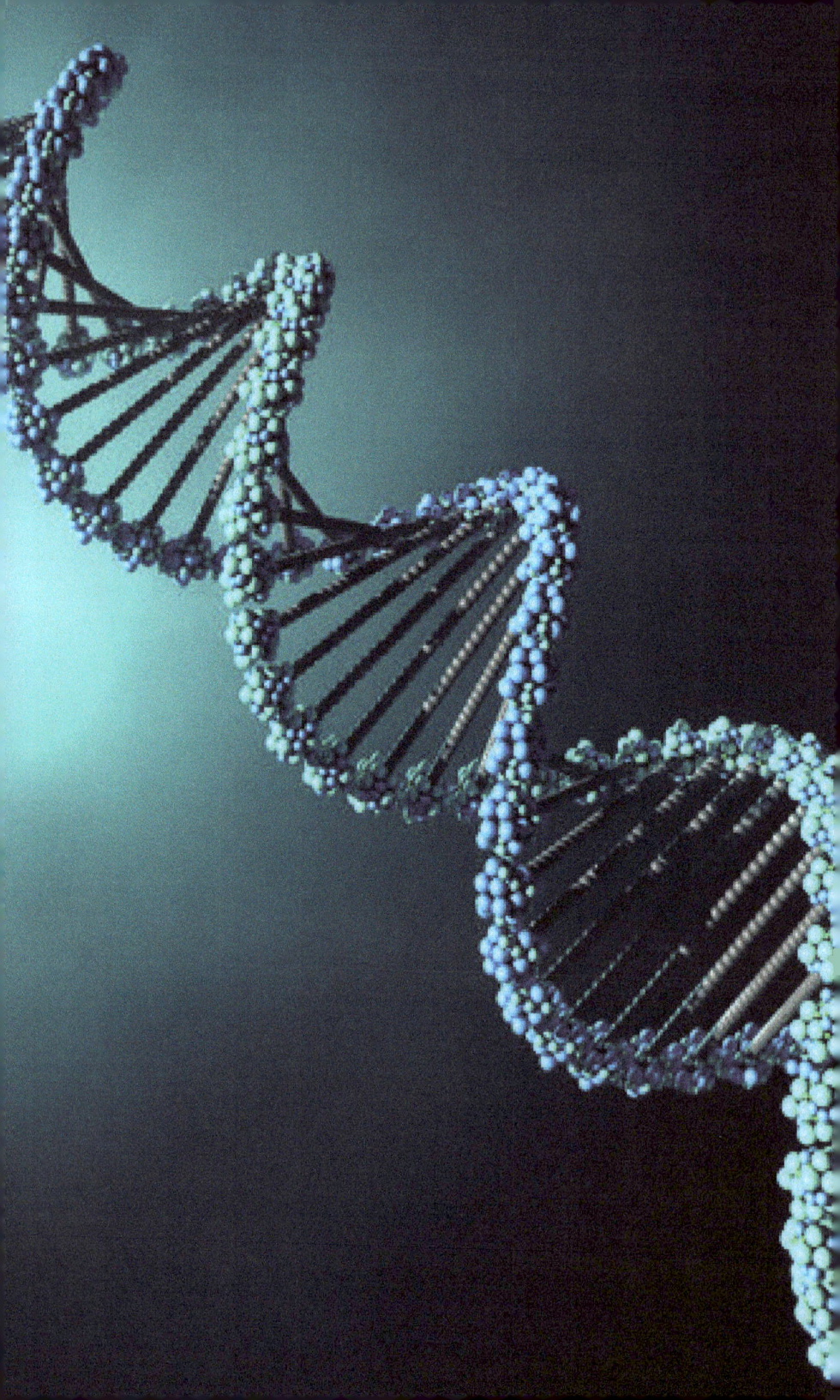

chapter 14

DNA

DNA. Those three little letters brought an end to the concept of evolution, for it is recognized throughout the world as the blueprint of life. DNA is the instruction book on the exact makeup of every single lifeform. DNA is for the body what a maintenance manual is for an automobile. Every part, every fitting, every electrical device, every chemical additive, and every engineering purpose is produced by the DNA code. It takes intelligence to program the codes to build the various organisms that live on planet earth.

> DNA is the instructional book on the exact makeup of every single life form.

Every lifeform contains its own unique master plan for life. The DNA not only directs the formation of each individual lifeform but also the repair of problem areas. Finally, DNA directs the procedures for reproduction so that the organism can continue its life's journey. *The only thing that an organism can become is what its DNA has programmed it to be.*

What is DNA and how is it formed? DNA stands for deoxyribonucleic (dee-OK-see-ri-bo-new-klee-ik) acid. It is the genetic information inside the cells of the body that helps make people who they are. DNA is the basic instructions for how to make your body, except these instructions come from two different sources. One set of instructions from your mother and a totally different set of instructions from your father.

These two sets of instructions form one set to make you. Because of the huge variety between people, no two DNA codes are the same. There will be similarities between identical twins, but they still have their own DNA code. Duplication of the genetic information occurs by the use of one DNA strand as a template for formation of a complementary strand. The duplication process starts at insemination of the cell and will continue until you die. It is the makeup of each strand that makes every strand of DNA unique, making each of us unique.

How unique are we? Each human being is separated by 6.4 million base pairs. This means that the chance that two people are genetically identical is 1/246,400,000, such a small number that it is essentially zero.

Consider the number of different kinds of fish that exist—saltwater and freshwater—and not only the different kinds of fish, but the numbers of the same kind of fish. It's just amazing! Next, do that same exercise with amphibians, reptiles, birds, and mammals, as well as all the different kinds of bugs and insects. I guess God could have left the bugs out of His creation but then what would the birds eat?

> Every plant and animal has its very own DNA.

Every plant and animal has its very own DNA. Included in the DNA is each individual characteristic that each type of animal needs to be effective in its environment. As another example, let's look at a spider's web. The spider can weave a web with several different kinds of webbing so they can catch their prey without getting stuck in their own web.

Another example would be snakes that are extremely poisonous, having either a neurotoxin which effects the nervous system when their prey is bitten, or a hemotoxin which attacks the blood in the circulatory system when bitten. There are also numerous defense systems like the speed of a cheetah, the bulk of a bear, the scent of a skunk, the quill of a porcupine, the chemical light display of a cuttlefish, the shock of an electric eel, and the numbers of animals with claws and fangs—all of these things are a result of the programming in their DNA.

In the end, each plant and animal will be whatever their DNA specifies them to be. The DNA will build its height, weight, size—big or little—for every fish, amphibian, reptile, bird, mammal, as well as the features of every human being.

Your DNA is clearly from the mind of God, because no man on earth could have dreamed up a storage device so complex that even in the 21st century we still only understand about 10% of the total function of the DNA. The more we look into DNA, the more we uncover a complex God. It is not the organism that determines the DNA but rather it is the DNA that determines the organism.

> Your DNA is clearly from the mind of God.

Next we will talk about how no species can turn into a different species. No one has ever seen anything turn into anything other than what its DNA originally created it to be. Evolution talks about the "missing link" or transitional animals or lifeforms like one that is half of one thing and half of another. Evolutionists are even today still looking for something they will never find.

POINTS TO PONDER

1. DNA is the blueprint for life.
2. DNA defines the objective for each living creature.
3. DNA makes a distinction between other life forms.

chapter 15

Transitional Forms

Years ago, it was believed that given enough time, one species of animal could completely transform into another form of animal. To prove this, the focus of the research became known as the search for the "missing link." The assumption was that there was a chain of lifeforms that evolved into another.

For instance, we have rats and we also have bats. If rats turned into bats over a period of time, the fossils would hold some evidence of the transition between the two animals. Given enough time, could a horse turn into a cow? The answer is no. Even when you have very similar animals such as a horse and a donkey, you can get an offspring which is a mule. But in 90% or more of the cases, the mule is sterile and cannot reproduce.

> The assumption was, given enough time, one animal could completely change into another form of animal.

What do the fossils say? The fossils give no indication that there is any organism that is half of one and half of another. Let's go back to the rat and the bat. If there was a transitional form of a half rat and half bat, how long could it live? It could neither run nor fly. It would neither have the means to escape danger, nor could it defend itself. Any other animal that is in mid-transition would face the same dilemma. The reason the fossils didn't contain any evidence of a transition is because the animals that were in transition would either have been eaten or unable to find food on their own. The other probability is that such transitional life forms simply did not exist.

> The fossils give no indication there is an organism that is half of this or that.

In the mid-1800s Charles Darwin visited the Galapagos Islands. While there, Darwin discovered that there were thirteen different kinds of finches on the islands. He noted that these little birds varied in color, size, and beak length. Darwin believed that the differences in the finches was due to variations in their habitats. To Darwin, the birds must have evolved from one original type of finch.

> If there was a transitional form of a half rat or half bat, how long could it live?

But the one thing that Darwin didn't note was that while he was focusing on the differences of the finches and how they must have evolved, they were still finches. The finches merely adapted to their changing environments. Adaptation has nothing to do with evolution. Animals learn how to adapt to changing conditions but they do not evolve into a different species than they were before. A finch will always be a finch. An eagle will always be an eagle. An ostrich will always be an ostrich. And a hummingbird will always be a hummingbird.

Birds of different species have no interest in other species. You will never see eagles hanging around with turkeys. It just doesn't happen. That's one reason someone once said, "Birds of a feather flock together." This is true with all animals, whether they be herds, flocks, packs, schools, swarms, or prides. The animals within these groups stay together, providing their members with security and companionship.

> Birds of a feather flock together

Nowhere at any time has there been any evidence that one species ever turned into another species. Even Darwin never offered any scientific proof that all organisms evolved from a common ancestor. Darwin's research supported the fact that small changes may occur over time, but never has one organism turned into another one. Adaptation is a part of life, but evolution is not.

> Nowhere at any time has there ever been any evidence that one species has turned into another species.

In the next chapter, we will be talking about precision. Precision is life's timing. We will talk about how creation shows that it was part of a grand design planned by the creator.

POINTS TO PONDER

1. Transitional lifeforms are nonexistent.
2. Transitional lifeforms only distract from the main objective.
3. Transitional lifeforms are a result of stretching the truth.

chapter 16

Precision

Let's suppose that we go on a walk through the forest one day. On our journey, we come across a pocket watch. Having never seen such an object, our casual glance of the object turns into a closer investigation of its function and purpose. We see that the object has 12 numbers on its face going from 1 to 12 in a "clockwise" display. It has three arrows all going the same direction but at different speeds.

The larger arrow travels the circumference every sixty seconds. The next size down arrow travels the circumference every minute. The smallest arrow makes the trip once per hour. To take the investigation even further, we open this object to expose an intricate display of gears and springs, all working together to make the object function every second, every minute, every hour of every day.

So what is the point here? If that scenario was true, and we were to find a pocket watch, there is no way one could think to himself that the watch must have grown there.

> **The intricacy of the workings of the watch with three distinct speeds: seconds, minutes, and hours, all working in precision, all by design.**
>
> **The timing is impeccable.**

Not only were all the pieces made and put together, but all the pieces work together in a precise manner. Every second, every minute and hour, every day, every week, every month, and every year—all function in our solar system, galaxy, and universe. We know down to the second exactly where everything will be. Precision in a pocket watch or the universe is no accident, it is only by design.

And did you know that the timing of a simple pocket watch can be synchronized to the timing of our solar system down to the exact second. The earth's orbit takes it completely around the sun in 365 days, or 52 weeks, or 12 months—exactly. This is due to the earth having a circular orbit versus an elliptical one. The same is true of the moon which is on a 30-day circular orbit around the earth. Precision in a pocket watch or the universal movement of the stars is no accident, it is by design. The timing is perfect.

> Make the object function every second, every minute, every hour of every day.

Precision timing is most beneficial when it's important to be on time and when it comes to athletic events or long-term travel—including space travel. The reason I included precision in our discussion is because it shows how detailed God can be, from the instantaneous creation to the long-term anticipated return of Christ, God is not confined to the concept of time because there is no time in heaven. But for our benefit time is important.

> Precision shows how detailed God can be.

Anyone who has a job has to report to work on time. In football the last two minutes of the game are often the most exciting. In basketball the last few seconds often determine the outcome of the game. More often than not, timing makes the difference. Precision timing is most beneficial when it's important to be on time. Timing is most important when it comes to athletic

> God is not confined to the concept of time.

events and long-term travel—including the space program.

Precision is a characteristic of God. The fact that God is precise is to our benefit. We then learn how to work together in a precise manner. The fact that the universe is precise in every way says that God is precise. It is a reflection that beholders of God see regularly. It is one way to show that God exists without actually seeing Him. We will see evidence of His existence through water in the next chapter.

POINTS TO PONDER

1. Precision works by design.
2. Precision is universal and orderly.
3. Precision is dependable and totally accurate.

chapter 17

Water

Water is essential to life on earth, but water itself is not living; it only makes life possible. Every living thing that we know of is dependent on water. So where did water come from? Researchers say that there may be water on the moon or perhaps on Mars. Scientists have searched the heavens and as far as we know, other than the Earth, the Moon and Mars, there are no other places in the heavens where water exists. So let's go back to our original question: Where did water come from—that colorless, odorless, and tasteless substance that makes life possible?

> Where did water come from?

This compound comes in three different forms: solid, liquid, and vapor. Does water make itself? If so, then how and when? We have never observed the process. We see the water cycle every day somewhere on earth that gives us clean water by recycling old water, but the process does not make new water.

> All the water that exists today has always existed.

Today if we use more water through farming and industry, it does not deplete the amount of water available. The truth is that all the water that exists today has always existed—no more, no less!

Water never increases or decreases in volume across the vast universe and is thus regarded as a rare commodity in the universe. It is also unique in the number of variations that are characteristics of this most valued compound. Water is made of two inanimate elements without being alive themselves. It is made up of two very similar atoms; one of oxygen, a very combustible atom, and two atoms of hydrogen which is a very explosive element. However, when these two combine, they form an effective means of fighting fires rather than feeding them, and has the ability to dissolve most substances.

Water can be an extremely destructive force capable of leveling anything that gets in its way, as evidenced by hurricanes, tsunamis, and flooding. Yet, water can be a refreshing mist that sustains life for both the animal and plant kingdoms. Water actively protects sea life by expanding when frozen rather than freezing and shrinking like all the other elements. Because it expands when frozen, the ice stays on top of the water. This enables fish and mammals that live in the water to safely swim under the ice without being caught in the ice.

> Water was there from the very beginning.

Water is important on a daily basis because man can only go for about three days without water. But better than that is fresh water! Fresh water goes through the water cycle and the natural filtering system and you can see and taste the difference. It is no wonder that we see so many different kinds of water on the shelves in the supermarket. And each company thinks their water is the best. The reason that we put water on our list of topics is because water is so important in our lives and the lives of all animals and plants. When God created the earth, water was the first element that was there from the very beginning.

> In the beginning, God created the heavens and the earth. And the earth was without form and void:

and darkness was on the face of the deep [water]. And the Spirit of God moved upon the face of the waters (Genesis 1:1-2).

Water itself is a product of genius thinking. Water doesn't make itself so the only other option is that it was created by the Creator, using two explosive elements to supply the earth with the most important ingredient in life. There is always an element of mystery when God is in the picture. I'll give you three examples.

> Water, itself, is a product of genius thinking.

The first one is a pearl. We have an oyster that has something that is irritating it. So to deal with the problem, the oyster begins to coat this object with a solution that covers the irritant with a smooth coating which becomes a pearl—something of great value. The irritant becomes an object of value.

Other examples are coal and oil. Great forests and numerous animals were buried by mud and debris during the Great Flood of Noah. Several months after the Flood, the water began to dissipate and dry land began to appear. Beneath the dry land, changes began to take place as a result of the flood. Great forests turned into coal beds and the remains of herds of animals turned into oil. Some coal mines have had to dig nearly a mile underground before they could access the coal; and some of the oil wells are being dug as deep as 40,000 feet in order to access the oil.

> Both coal and oil are products of the Great Flood

Both coal and oil are products of the Great Flood—and the reason they are called fossil fuels. A catastrophic event like Noah's Flood resulted in the making of some tremendously useful products. Both coal and oil are found on all seven continents—thus another reason why the Great Flood had to be a world-wide event.

> Beneath the dry land changes began to take place as a result of the Flood.

The third example of when God is

involved in a mystery is in the making of a diamond. Sometimes the weight, pressure, and heat turned the forests into coal, and in some places the heat and pressure were so great that it turned the coal into diamonds. So once again, something that was catastrophic turned into something of great value which is extremely beneficial—we burn coal and we wear diamonds.

> Pressure and heat turned the forests into coal and in some places it turned the coal into diamonds.

In this chapter, we have discussed how important water is to life—it is life's thirst quencher. Where there is water—there is life. Where there is no water—there is no life. Water is the amazing creation of Almighty God. In our next chapter, we will be discussing the ingenious design of the water cycle.

> Water is life's thirst quencher.

POINTS TO PONDER

1. Water is necessary for life.
2. Water is abundant on earth.
3. Water is a universal commodity; it has many uses.

chapter 18

Fresh Water

As I mentioned before, some believe there may be water on the Moon or maybe on Mars, but there is no evidence to dogmatically make that assertion. To do so would be speculation, not science. As I also said previously, we know water exists here on earth but we are unsure if it exists anywhere else in the universe. Because there is water on Earth, there can be life on Earth. These are facts. So, where did water come from? It definitely didn't evolve.

> **Water is distributed throughout the Earth by the water cycle, the wind, storms and gravity.**

What else do we have to consider? We have already talked about water, but let's take this one step further. What if there was no water on the earth? We have already stated that if there was no water there would be no life. But what if there was water, but there was no way to distribute the water to where it was needed?

What if there was no water cycle? And, what if there was water, but the water just sat where it was without any movement—it was just stagnant? We take for granted the water cycle, but the water cycle plays a major part in providing fresh water every day for everyone in every part of the earth.

> Because there is water on Earth, there can be life on Earth.

So what about water evaporation? Water turns into a vapor and rises upward to the sky to be carried about by the winds. The vapor condenses and the coolness of the atmosphere causes the vapor to turn back into a liquid. The then heavy accumulation of water in the clouds causes the water to fall back to the earth as rain or snow.

This is precipitation and the third stage of the water cycle which represents the distribution plan to provide fresh water for people, plants, and animals all over the earth. Without the water cycle, both people and plants would struggle—especially plants because they are stationary in one place and cannot go and get water.

> The Moon is another part of God's water cycle.

There is one more contributor to the fresh water plan and that is the Moon. As the Moon travels around the Earth, it causes the tides to rise and fall. The tides move the water in and out of ports and inlets so the water doesn't become stagnant. The Moon is another part of the water cycle that we often forget about. Without the Moon, life on earth would be much different.

We have discussed how fresh water is the result of a highly efficient water cycle. The water evaporates, turns into a vapor and rises into the sky. There is the coolness of the atmosphere which causes the condensed water vapor and turns it into a liquid and then it falls back to the ground. Much of the precipitation falls on the mountains and goes down through the rocks to filter our water. In our next chapter we will be talking about clean air and its importance to our health.

POINTS TO PONDER

1. Fresh water is a result of good planning and a great design.
2. Fresh water comes from a natural filtering system.
3. Fresh water meets the needs of both plants and animals.

chapter 19

Clean Air

> **Winds gain strength and become like giant vacuum cleaners.**

Just as there has to be a means to make fresh water for everyone, there is a means to make clean air. We recognize the benefits of the wind throughout the earth. As the Earth travels around the sun at a 23 degree angle, the air at the poles slips down to fill the gaps left by the hot air at the equator. The hot air at the equator then makes its way to the poles. Often, these winds gain strength and become like giant vacuum cleaners that churn the air into tornados or hurricanes.

These storms also produce rain and clear the dirt and debris from an area. As the winds and rain travel through an area, we can literally smell the new clean air. One might think that those storms are a high price to pay for clean air, but we have to remember it's a big job to do. Life will go on with cleaner air, making it a little easier to breathe. It's like cleaning a house.

Plants also contribute to the clean air factor by taking in carbon dioxide and producing oxygen in return. This whole process works by design—not by accident. If it wasn't for the two poles (one at the north and one at the south), and the warm air at the equator, along with the 23 degree tilt (as well as the winds that help distribute the air), the Earth's atmosphere would be quite different. And life—well, who knows!

> This whole process works by design - not by accident.

The whole process of obtaining clean air is directly from the mind of God. In order for there to be clean air, there had to be an urgent need and, indeed, there was. Without clean air, life on earth would be difficult. But God had a plan.

"For thus says the Lord who created the heavens, God Himself who formed the earth and made it; He has established it, He created it not in vain, He formed it to be inhabited" (Isaiah 45:18). Clean air is one concept that makes the earth inhabitable. Clean air is God's plan to help people and enable them to live a healthy life.

> "He formed it to be inhabited."

Clean air is a product of God's ongoing process to care for His creation. He didn't forget His promise to provide for the needs of His people. This is also an activity that is ongoing every day for as long as the earth is around.

In the next chapter, we will discuss something called the Biosphere II which was built as a prototype for possible space travel. It was patterned after Biosphere I which is the earth. The program which was going to last two years ended after six months. Things didn't work out exactly as they had planned but much was learned through the experiment.

POINTS TO PONDER

1. Clean air is often the result of catastrophic storms.
2. Clean air is the result of a great design.
3. Clean air is necessary for a healthy life.

chapter 20

Biosphere II

In the 1980s the University of Arizona acquired some land and built what they called Biosphere II. The earth was designated to be Biosphere I, but the intent was for Biosphere II to be as much like Biosphere I as possible. The building was a very impressive 3.14 acre structure with the thought of using the facility as a model for research into sustaining life on earth, identifying everything that would be necessary for life to exist, as well as a possible structure to serve as a base for space exploration training.

> A model for research into sustaining life on Earth.

Inside this elaborate building were five distinctly different habitats engineered to see how each responded to certain stimuli. There was an ocean, a mangrove wetlands, a tropical rainforest, a savanna grasslands, and a fog desert. The atmosphere in the biosphere was controlled by a massive unit.

> Everything was patterned after life on Earth.

This beneficial study was to last two years and was to be run by eight "bionauts." They were to process their own food, plant and harvest their own plants, and recycle everything they could. Unfortunately, the study only lasted six months. Even though everything was patterned after life on earth, things started to go wrong.

First of all, the bees died. Without bees, there was no pollination. Without pollination, there would be no fruit leading to a shortage of food. With only eight bionauts, there wasn't enough carbon dioxide for the plants to breathe which, in turn, caused the oxygen levels to get out of control. There were no winds in the building, so large trees were never forced to stand their ground by digging their roots deeper and deeper. As a result, trees began to fall down.

The intent to build a structure after the original design of Biosphere I shows the difference between the two builders. Biosphere I is perfect. Biosphere II's efforts were noble but far from the creative ability of the Master Creator and sustainer of life on earth. Today, researchers still use the building for research and development of programs that will help colonize places in outer space. The world of Biosphere I remains under control because that is how it was designed to function.

> They needed to think about how bees thrive.

In reality, Biosphere II never had a chance to have all the advantages of Biosphere I. Having bees was a good start but they needed to think about how bees thrive. They not only needed pollen but they needed all the materials to make the hive and the instincts to reproduce a queen bee in order to continue life in the hive.

They needed other animals to provide enough carbon dioxide to keep plants alive. There were no storms in the Biosphere. Lightning produces nitrogen which plants need in order to grow and develop. No nitrogen—no growth. No storms—no action to force the trees to grow roots deep in the soil so the trees can grow and anchor themselves so they don't fall over. There were too many things that were missing which kept the operation of the Biosphere from being successful.

It was a good plan, however, and a good learning

experience. The greatest benefit of the challenge was that it made the people who ran the experiment appreciate the intellect and creativity of the creator of Biosphere I.

As I mentioned before, Biosphere II was erected to study the possibility of building a similar structure for space exploration. There would be a number of bugs to work out but that could happen over a period of time. There would need to be soil from earth so plants could have the nutrients for the plants to thrive. Having a good supply of fresh water is a must for both people and plants. The most purchased item in the States every day is toilet paper. There should be an abundance of that. This is just a small but very important list to get somewhere in outer space.

If you want to see what Biosphere I has to offer, read the next chapter and you will be amazed at what God can do. He created the perfect planet.

POINTS TO PONDER

1. Biosphere II was a great idea.
2. Biosphere II's expectations were high.
3. Biosphere II's plans were woefully inept.

chapter 21

The Perfect Planet

Let's look at the bigger picture. The earth is the perfect size. If the earth was any bigger, the gravity would be stronger and would completely change the atmosphere as we know it. If the earth was any smaller, the gravity would be less and again, the atmosphere would be completely changed. If the earth was any closer to the sun, the earth would be too hot and intolerable for life to exist. Any further from the sun, the earth would be too cold for life to exist. So the earth is the perfect size and distance from the sun.

> The earth is the perfect size and distance from the sun.

The earth is at a 23 degree tilt which is unique when we compare it to the other planets in our solar system. This tilt gives the earth four distinct seasons so there is a spring time for life to renew itself. Summer is a time for growing and maturing. Fall is a time for harvest. Winter is a time for rest. All four hemispheres are affected in some way during the earth's trip around

> Evolution is not based on scientific fact.

the sun. By way of comparison, Mars' tilt is the closest to Earth's with a 25 degree tilt.

You have been presented with facts which are indisputable. There are no arguments that can challenge the validity of what has been written so far. This book has been written for those who are sincere seekers of truth about the beginning of life. Even though no one was there when things on earth came into existence, we have enough scientific information to establish credible examples that an intelligent being created an intelligent world.

And in reality, evolution is not a viable theory because there is not one fact to support it. All the facts point to a Creator, not because I think so or because it's what I believe. Research for yourself what evolution teaches and compare it to what you have just read. Can you really believe that everything is a result of a big accident that happened by chance? What is important is that you know and believe the truth. Ask yourself questions and do the research. Truth is not afraid of questions. On the contrary, truth welcomes a challenge.

> All the facts point to a Creator.

We are not talking about a religious debate, but a scientific inquiry into the facts. If one is going to believe in something, one must make sure they can defend their position. I have written this book to present the truth so you can know it. I chose the title of this book to be *Irrefutable* because the facts are the facts. Facts do not change. The validity of facts cannot be questioned.

> Earth is indeed a perfect planet.

Earth is indeed the perfect planet and a perfect reflection of the glory of God. The existence of planet earth has been designed and created by our Creator who you will meet in the next chapter. Earth is the perfect planet because of all the attributes that are featured in the pages of this book such as:

- The size and distance from the sun
- The atmosphere has just the right elements that

make breathing without masks possible
- The 23 degree tilt of the earth
- The four seasons
- Fresh water
- Water cycles
- Clean air
- The winds that aid in moving clouds and clean the air
- Abundance of food
- Time
- Gravity
- Plants that give off oxygen

Earth is the perfect planet and in the next chapter we will meet our Creator—God—who made it that way.

POINTS TO PONDER

1. The Earth is the perfect planet because of a perfect plan.
2. The Earth is the perfect planet because it supports and sustains life.
3. The Earth is the perfect planet because it is unique in all the universe—there is none other like it.

chapter *22*

The Creator

Now that we have established that there is a Creator behind the universe we live in, I want to take a little time to share with you about that Creator. As stated previously, all the facts presented in this book point to there being a Creator. Everything was created for the benefit of humanity so they can have a relationship with the Creator who we address as God. The Bible says that God loves all people and wants us to live with Him after this life's journey is over. Most of what we know about the Creator can be found in the Bible.

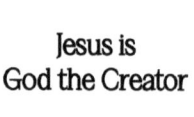

Jesus is God the Creator

We know that God has the ability to create whatever He wants, whenever He wants. That is who He is—that is His character. That is why there are so many things in existence, and such a wide array of possibilities. There are so many more attributes of our Creator that time will not permit me to cover them here, but they include the means by which creation was created. The Bible simply says that God spoke the world—and all things in it—into existence. That is something no mere human being would be able to do, and we must be careful not to limit what God desires to do.

Psalms 33:6, 9 says, "By the Word of the Lord were the Heavens made, their starry host by the breath of His mouth. For He spoke, and it came to be; he commanded, and it stood firm." In Genesis 1:3, He said, "Let there be light, and there was light." Wherever we look in creation, we see God spoke into existence everything He desired. The Bible says in John 1:3, "Through Him all things were made; without Him nothing was made that has been made." Colossians 1:16 says, "For by Him [Jesus Christ] all things were created; things in heaven and on earth, visible and invisible … all things were created by Him and for Him."

> By the Word of the Lord were the heavens made.

In order to sustain life, God created the earth perfect for life. God created the water cycle to continue to have fresh water, as well as a way to constantly have clean air—both of which are important for life on earth. A group from the University of Arizona tried to duplicate God's creativity in providing a place to sustain life. They called this place Biosphere II, the earth being Biosphere I. What was to operate for two years only lasted for six months.

> It is Jesus who is the creator and sustainer of life on earth.

Again, it was God who made the difference. It was God who made earth the perfect place for life. Jesus is the creator who brought everything into existence. It is Jesus who is the creator and sustainer of life on earth. Paul wrote in Colossians 1:16-17,

> For by Him [Jesus] all things were created that are in heaven and that are on earth, visible and invisible, whether thrones or dominions or principalities or powers. All things were created through him and for Him. And He is before all things, and in Him all things consist.

Creation is extremely important because it shows that God is the Creator who has no limits. Ephesians 3:20 says, "Now unto Him (Jesus) who is able to do exceeding abundantly

above all that we can ask or think or imagine."
Now
Unto Him (Jesus)
Who is Able
To Do
Exceeding
Above
All
That We Ask
Or Think

Now unto Him that is *able* ...

Now unto Him that is able *to do* ...

Now unto Him that is able to do *exceeding* ...

Now unto Him that is able to do exceeding *above* ...

Now unto Him that is able to do exceeding above *all that we ask* ...

Now unto Him that is able to do exceeding above all that we ask *or think* ...

Now you've had a chance to meet the Creator who brought everything into being. In the next chapter titled "The Savior," you can meet Him. He wants to be your Savior. Please trust Him and believe that He is God who will save you, keep you, defend you, and protect you—that's what His name means. Believe Him—trust Him—know Him. Do that now.

POINTS TO PONDER

1. God created everything visible and invisible.
2. God created everything by voice command.
3. God created everything to sustain life.

chapter 23

The Savior

The rest of the story is amazing. God the Creator is perfect in character and lives in a single place we call heaven. The Bible says that we are sinful and do not deserve to go to heaven, but because of His great love for us, God took on flesh and was born in a little town called Bethlehem. The Savior became a baby and grew up as a man who was called Jesus.

> The empty cross, the empty tomb - believe it!

Heaven is a perfect place, which is why we cannot go there because of our sin. Our sinfulness is not to be compared with others' sins but is rather compared to God's perfection. Since we are not as good as God, God came to earth, lived a perfect sinless life for us, died for our sins, was buried, and rose again. God offers eternal life to those who believe in Jesus as their Savior. They are saved from the consequences of sin so they can have eternal life and live in Heaven.

> God offers eternal life to those who believe.

It is Jesus who is also our Savior.

The Bible says that the wages of sin is death (Romans 3:23). The Bible also says that all have sinned and fall short of the glory of God (Romans 3:23). We all sin. We may think we are pretty good but we are not as good as God—and that is the issue.

Heaven isn't just a good place—it is a perfect place and you have to be perfect to go there. We are not perfect so how can we go there? God has an answer for that too. When you believe in Jesus as your Savior, God then declares you perfect. Your sins are forgiven and you are justified—just as if you'd never sinned. You are declared totally righteous and when you die, you will go to heaven and enjoy eternal life. The moment you believe, the Holy Spirit enters you and you are sealed—like they used to do with scrolls a long time ago. That seal on the scroll was the guarantee it would get it to its destination and that it was from the person who owned the seal. The Bible says the Holy Spirit is our guarantee that we will get to heaven. Ephesians 1:13, 14 says,

> In Him you also trusted, after you heard the word of truth, the gospel of your salvation; in whom also, having believed, you were sealed with the Holy Spirit of promise, who is the guarantee of our inheritance until the redemption of the purchased possession, to the praise of His glory.

God/Jesus came to earth as a baby and grew up to be a man. He lived a perfect sinless life for us. He took the punishment for our sins, the sin of every person who has or will ever live. He died on the cross, was buried, and three days later rose from the dead. He had power over sin and death. His offer of eternal life—if we believe that he died for us—is still available if we simply believe.

That is good news—that is the Gospel—believing that God is able to deliver us and declare us perfect so we can spend eternity with Him. The Bible says, "Most assuredly, I say to you, He who believes in me has eternal life" (John 6:47). Note that Jesus used the present tense in that verse. Anyone who believes *has* eternal life right now.

> "He who believes in Me has eternal life."

Believing in Christ is not only what you must do, it's the

only thing you can do if you want to know for sure where you will spend eternity after you die. Ephesians 2:8-9 states,

> For by grace (getting what you don't deserve) are you saved (from the wrath of God) through faith (simply believing), and not of yourselves (it was nothing you did on your own), it is the gift of God (eternal life is God's gift to believers); not of works (not by doing good things), lest any man (any person, should boast (brag about their effort to do things for God). (Words in parentheses are my addition and interpretation.)

Jesus was not just a good man or good teacher. Jesus was not just a good prophet. Jesus is God the Creator. Jesus is God who became a man. Jesus lived a perfect life for us. Jesus died on the cross to take the punishment for our sins. Jesus rose from the dead, proving He has power over both sin and death. Jesus offers eternal life to anyone who would believe in Him because of what He has done on the cross.

> **Jesus died on the cross for our sins.**

The Bible says that we should believe in the name of Jesus:

> "He that believes on Him is not condemned: but He that believes not is condemned already, because he has not believed in the name of the Son of God" (John 3:18).

Believing in the "name" cannot happen unless you know what His name means. The New Testament was written in Greek so the writers used the Greek name Jesus for the Hebrew name Joshua. Joshua is a contraction of two Hebrew words:

- Jehovah – God's personal name
- Yahsha – which means saves, keeps, defends, and protects.

So, when you believe in the name of the Son of God, you believe that Jesus is God who will:

Save you …

Keep you …

Defend you ...

And protect you.

These things I have written unto you that believe on the name of the Son of God; that you may know that you eternal life, and that you may believe on the name of the Son of God (1 John 5:13).

"Neither is there salvation in any other; for there is no other name under heaven given among men, whereby we must be saved" (Acts 4:12).

Wherefore God also has highly exalted Him, and given Him a name which is above every name (Philippians 2:9).

Being made so much better than the angels, He has by inheritance obtained a more excellent name than they (Hebrews 1:4).

One day, I shared this offer of eternal life to a young lady. Her response was, "it seems too simple." It is simple but profound.

There is a story in the Old Testament that deals with that same concept of salvation through miraculous means. We find in Numbers 21:4-9 a passage that talks about a time when the people of Israel ran out of water and began to complain about their situation to God and Moses. In order to show the people that they shouldn't complain, God sent snakes into the camp. If the people were bitten, they would die.

> The symbol of the bronze snake on a pole is where our medical symbol came from.

God spoke to Moses and told him to make a bronze snake and put it up on a pole. He instructed the people that if they were bitten, they could look at the bronze snake and they would live. They didn't have to touch it or do anything else, they just had to look and they would be healed. It was simple, not complex. (The symbol of the bronze snake on a pole is where our medical symbol comes from that is used today on ambulances, doctor's offices and many other places.)

John 3 has the same illustration in it. It promises that anyone who looked at the bronze snake would live. Also in the Gospel of John it says if you believe, you have eternal life. If you don't believe, it will be a sad day when you die.

The evidence is clear. The truth has been revealed. All you have to do is believe it! Why don't you just do that right now, in the quietness of your own mind? God knows your thoughts. Take God at His Word—believe Him! The empty cross says the work is finished. The empty tomb says He has risen to offer us eternal life.

> The truth has been revealed.

The next chapter gives more details on creation. Don't stop reading now. Complete your task and read how and what Christ has done for us. We will also answer the question, "How and when did life begin?" God spoke and things came into existence. That's how. When did it happen? In the very beginning, when God created Adam and Eve.

POINTS TO PONDER

1. The Savior (Jesus) left His home in Heaven for the purpose of dying for our sins.
2. He took the punishment for our sins and offers a pardon—forgiveness—from sins to anyone who would trust Him as their Savior.
3. Jesus was crucified for our sins. He was buried—His mission was finished. He rose from the dead—proving He had power over sin and death. He offers eternal life if we simply believe it.

chapter 24

Creation

While the book of Genesis gives us the most details of Creation, other books also give us some insight into the creation process. Psalms 33:6, 9 says that, "By the Word of the Lord were the Heavens made and all the host of them by the breath of His mouth; for He spoke and it was done, He commanded and it stood fast." So things were spoken into existence and whatever God wanted was done.

> **Things were spoken into existence.**

As humans, we have a hard time understanding that. We have to take what is available and make things from that, whereas God can make something out of nothing and speak it into existence. We have the tendency to place limitations on God based on our abilities or lack thereof; but God is God and He is not limited by anything.

Genesis 1:1 says, "In the beginning God created the Heavens and the Earth." The *Heaven* he is probably talking about is the angelic realm because the book of Job 38:7 says, "When the morning stars sang together and all the Sons of God shouted for joy." Morning stars refer to angels. So when they saw the Earth for the first time, they shouted for joy. God and the angels must live in another dimension, a spiritual realm which is much different from the physical realm. The physical realm was dark which is why one of the first things God made was light.

> He formed the Earth to be inhabited.

Genesis 1:2 says, "And the Earth was without form and void." *Without form* means this earth hadn't taken on the sphere shape yet; and *void* means that there was no life yet. Isaiah 45:18 says, "For thus says the Lord that created the Heavens; God Himself that formed the Earth and made it: He has established it, He created it not in vain, He formed it to be inhabited."

Genesis 1:2 continues, "And darkness was upon the face of the deep." Deep refers to the water on Earth. Genesis 1:3 says, "And the Spirit of God moved upon the face of the waters." The word moved is defined as brooded, which is what a chicken does to keep her eggs warm. Her stomach vibrates and the friction causes the stomach to warm and, therefore, the eggs stay warm. It's a picture of what the Holy Spirit does to aid in the life process. Genesis 1:3 continues, "And God said, 'Let there be light' and there was light." In the Scriptures, *light* and *truth* are synonymous.

> In the Scriptures, *light* and *truth* are synonymous.

> Genesis 1:4 – And God saw the light, that it was good; and God divided the light from the darkness.
>
> Genesis 1:5 – God called the light Day and the darkness He called Night. So the evening and the morning were the first day.
>
> Genesis 1:6 – Then God said, "Let there be a firmament in the midst of the waters, and let it divide the waters from the waters."
>
> Genesis 1:7 – Thus God made the firmament, and divided the waters which were under the firmament from the waters which were above the firmament; and it was so.

Ever wonder where all the rain came from to flood the earth over the tops of mountains? When God divided the waters above from the waters below, it required that a lot of water remain on earth and the rest of the water went up in the sky to form a water canapé around the earth. Picture if you will a softball inside a basketball. When it rained during Noah's flood, all the water up in the sky poured down on the earth and all the land was flooded. Plus, a lot of water shot up from the ground through subterranean reserves.

Genesis 1:8 – And God called the firmament Heaven. So the evening and the morning were the second day.

Genesis 1:9 – "And God said, 'Let the waters under the heavens be gathered together into one place, and let the dry land appear,' and it was so."

> "God saw that it was good."

Genesis 1:10 – And God called the dry land 'Earth'; and the gathering together of the waters He called 'Seas.' And God saw that it was good.

Genesis 1:11 – "And God said, 'Let the earth bring forth grass, the herb that yields seed, and the fruit tree that yields fruit according to its kind, whose seed is in itself on the earth'; and it was so."

Genesis 1:13 – So the evening and the morning were the third day.

Genesis 1:14 – "Let there be lights in the firmament of the heavens to divide the day from the night; and let them be for signs and seasons, for days and years;"

Genesis 1:15 – "And let them be for lights in the firmament of the heavens to give light on the earth"; and it was so.

> "Let them be for signs and seasons, days and years."

Genesis 1:19 – So the evening

and the morning were the fourth day.

Genesis 1:20 – Then God said, "Let the waters abound with an abundance of living creatures, and let birds fly above the earth across the face of the firmament of the heavens."

Creation is the method which God used to bring things into existence. But the crown of creation is man. When Jesus created man, He created him in His own image. In the next chapter, we will discuss the creation continued. God loves to create because that's His character. His very nature is to create—from all the animals you see at the zoo to all the great dinosaurs. Creation brought life into this world.

POINTS TO PONDER

1. The goal of creation is to glorify God.
2. The crown of creation was man.
3. Creation was an outlet for a creative God.

chapter 25

Creation Continued

Let's continue our look at the Creation account in Genesis:

Genesis 1:21 – So God created great sea creatures and every living thing that moves, with which the waters abounded, according to their kind, and every winged bird according to its kind. And God saw that it was good.

Genesis 1:23 – So the evening and the morning were the fifth day.

Genesis 1:24 – Then God said, "Let the earth bring forth the living creature according to its kind: cattle and creeping thing and beast of the earth, each according to its kind"; and it was so.

Genesis 1:26 – Then God said, "Let Us make man in Our image, according to Our likeness; let them have dominion over the fish of the sea, over the birds of the air, and over the cattle,

> "God saw and behold it was very good."

over all the earth and over every creeping thing that creeps on the earth."

Genesis 1:31 – Then God saw everything that He had made, and indeed it was very good. So the evening and the morning were the sixth day.

> All things were made by Him.

Genesis 2:1-2 – Thus the heavens and the earth, and all the host of them, were finished. And on the seventh day God ended His work which He had done, and He rested on the seventh day from all His work which He had done.

These are the days of creation and the events of each day. The climax was the creation of man who was created in God's image. Man was the crown of God's creation.

John 1:1 says – In the beginning was the Word, and the Word was with God, and the Word was God.

John 1:2 says – He was in the beginning with God.

John 1:3 says – All things were made through Him, and without Him nothing was made that was made.

Romans 1:18 says – For the wrath of God is revealed from heaven against all ungodliness and unrighteousness of men, who suppress the truth in unrighteousness of men.

Romans 1:19 – Because what may be known of God is manifest in them, for God has shown it to them.

Romans 1:20 – For since the creation of the world His invisible attributes are clearly seen, being understood by the things that are made, even His eternal power and Godhead, so that they are without excuse.

Colossians 1:15 says – He is the image of the invisible God, the firstborn over all creation.

Colossians 1:16 – For by Him all things were created that are in heaven and that are on earth, visible and invisible, whether thrones or dominions or principalities or powers. All things were created through Him and for Him.

Colossians 1:17 – And He is before all things, and in Him all things consist.

Hebrews 1:1 – God, who at various times and in various ways spoke in time past to the fathers by the prophets,

Hebrews 1:2 – Has in these last days spoken to us by His Son, whom He has appointed heir of all things, through whom also He made the worlds.

> His invisible attributes are clearly seen.

Another question that would rank as one of the most important questions is: What came first? The chicken or the egg? The things that were created can all go back in the box. Adam and Eve are on the scale. But both Adam and Eve were created as young adults, indicating that all living things were created with an appearance of age like Adam and Eve, including trees with fruit on them already.

> "By Him all things consist."

The sun and moon and stars were created instantly, but immediately functioned as we know them to do today. After all, what does a 30-minute 20-year-old look like? He would look like a 20-year-old man even though he has been on Earth only 30 minutes. The stars would look like they were a million light years away—but they would only be 30 minutes old.

> All things were created with an appearance of age.

POINTS TO PONDER

1. The divine hand in creation is evident to all who look for it.
2. God made creation adequate to meet all needs.
3. Creation is the handiwork of the Creator.

chapter 26

Creation Completed

As I have mentioned before, God loves to create. We see this in the number of things He created—from the greatness of the universe down to the single-celled critters. And every created thing has a purpose. We might wonder, *Why in the world did God create ants?* The Bible has the answer for that. We find it in the book of Proverbs 6:6-9 which says,

> "Go to the ant, you sluggard. Consider her ways and be wise; which having no captain, overseer or ruler, provides her supplies in the summer and gathers her food in the harvest. How long will you slumber, O sluggard? When will you rise from your sleep?"

Here the writer uses an ant to teach a lesson from the working nature of the ants. The Bible is full of other lessons like that from nature. Matthew 10:29 says, "Are not two sparrows sold for a copper coin? And not one of them falls to the ground apart from your Father's will, but the very hairs of your head are numbered. Do not fear therefore, you are of more value than many sparrows." God uses His creative world and written Word to carry His message to all.

We find in John 2:1-10 the account of when Jesus turned water into wine. In the New Testament, the Holy Spirit and

> "The very hairs on your head are numbered."

water are synonymous. We see in this passage Christ's first public miracle of turning the water into wine, through which He sent a message and gave indication of His creative powers. This miracle that occurred was at a wedding in Cana of Galilee, and the mother of Jesus was there. Jesus and his disciples were also invited to the wedding. When they ran out of wine, Jesus' mother said to Him, "They have no wine." His mother said to the servants, "Whatever He says to you, do it." So He told them to fill water pots with water.

Through this miracle, Jesus confirmed His deity by taking water, accelerating the process of the time it would take to grow the grape vines, harvest the grapes, press the grapes, and collect the grape juice and age it—in order to turn it into wine. Jesus took what He had and turned the water into wine.

So, when we talk about creation being complete, we are saying that the creative works are finished—no new creation, no new animals, no new plants. What is Jesus doing now? According to the Bible, right now Jesus is preparing a place for believers to spend eternity with Him in heaven.

John 14:2 says, "In my Father's house are many mansions, if it were not so, I would have told you. I go to prepare a place for you." First Peter 1:4 states, "To an inheritance incorruptible and undefiled and that does not fade away, reserved in heaven for you" (this is addressed to believers). And you can know for sure that you are going to heaven. First John 5:13 says, "I have written to you who believe in the name of the Son of God, that you may know that you have eternal life."

POINTS TO PONDER

1. Trust in the Creator; His way is the right way.
2. Truth is self-evident. You know it when you see it.
3. Good questions can help us focus on the creativity of the Creator.

Conclusion

After reviewing the facts it's easy to see how they all point to a Creator. It's kind of like:

>Water is wet.
>
>Fire is hot.
>
>Dogs bark.
>
>Birds fly.
>
>Fish swim.

What we have learned is that truth is self-evident. You kind of know when someone or something is truth or not. One of the most confounding questions was uttered to Jesus by Pilate when he asked, "What is truth?" When you stand before a judge they will ask you, "Will you tell the truth, the whole truth, and nothing but the truth, so help you God?" So truth is important and is a great start for a book.

> "What is truth?"

Next come the facts. The facts should support the truth. They are independent and unbiased. Nothing is important because nothing points to a Creator better than anything. Nothing can't stop a Creator from creating. The rock plays a big part in the recognition of a Creator because the inanimate cannot produce life. Life must come from a life giver.

Evolution misses the boat much like those who missed the ark back in Noah's day. They were bad to the bone and walked away from God and all He had to offer them. Time is something that God cannot give to you because God doesn't exist in the realm of time—He is eternal. He had no beginning and will never end. He offers eternal life to those who will believe in Him as Savior.

The wrath of God is reserved for those who reject God and the good things God offers. In Noah's day, the people rejected God and ended up missing the ark. Around 325 years later, God helped the people disperse by dividing the continents. In due time, a professor from the University of Chicago tried to create life in a science lab. He fell short of creating life because only God can create life.

We learned that good questions can help us focus on the creativity of God. When God created Adam, He gave Adam nine different systems to help maintain his well-being. Along the way, we discussed DNA and its purpose in providing for the continued existence of all living creatures: plants, animals, and man.

Evolutionists need a bridge in order to explain how certain species have turned into different species. There is no bridge to cross from one species to a different species; and only God can make something different than how it was created. It is God who programs DNA to perpetuate what He has started. Precision is one of the characteristics of God and it was God who programmed the timing of seconds … minutes … hours … days … weeks … months … and years. Therefore, we can count on everything being right on time, according to God's perfect plan.

God created the earth so that it is perfectly suited to sustain life. He created the water cycle to continue to have fresh water, as well as a way to constantly have clean air—both of which are important for life on earth. A group from the University of Arizona tried to replicate God's creativity by building a place to sustain life. They called it the Biosphere II (the Earth being Biosphere I).

What was to operate for two years only lasted for six months because it is God who is the Creator and Sustainer of Life. It is God who made the earth the perfect place for life. Jesus is the Creator who brought everything into existence. Jesus is also our Savior.

The Bible says that the wages of sin is death (see Romans 3:23). The Bible also says that all have sinned and fall short of the glory of God (see Romans 3:23). We all sin. We might think we are pretty good but we are not nearly as good as God and that is the issue. Heaven isn't just a good place, it is perfect place and you have to be perfect to go there. As stated, none of us are perfect.

Therefore, God/Jesus came to earth as a baby and grew up to be a man. He lived a perfect sinless life and took the punishment for our sins. He would die on the cross and be buried; and three days later He rose from the dead, proving that He had power over sin and death. And He has offered us eternal life if we simply believe that He did that for us. If we receive his gift of eternal life, we also believe that He has declared us perfect and we will go to heaven to be with Him when we die.

That's the Gospel, the good news. Believe it! The Bible says, "Most assuredly I say to you, he who believes in me has eternal life" (author's note: look at the present tense; *has* indicates right now). Believing in Christ is not only the thing you must do, it's the only thing you can do. Ephesians 2:8-9 says,

> For by grace (getting what you don't deserve) you have been saved (from the wrath of God) through faith (just believing), and that not of yourselves (nothing you did on your own), it is the gift of God (you don't pay for your own gift), not of works (not of doing good deeds), lest anyone should boast (lest any man should brag about what you did to earn God's gift). All parenthetical entries are mine and not part of God's word; they are there to help explain the meaning.)

You can know for sure that you have eternal life before you die. The Bible says, "These things I have written to you who believe that you may know that you have eternal life" (1 John 5:13).

Personal Note

People in Christian circles talk about "calling" or receiving a "call." It's interesting that everybody receives not one but two calls from God. The first and most important one is a calling to salvation. God's love is real and He offers salvation to anyone who will respond to His call. He invites you to have eternal life through Jesus. This call is personal and to you, the individual. Answer the call. God is waiting.

The second "call" is to believers and it is the call to service. God has given believers special talents to use in order to build His kingdom and serve others. God does not demand participation but He does offer blessings when believers are actively involved in the process. Take time to share what God has done for you. You have talents that you can use to honor the Lord, and encourage unbelievers. This is the second call. Don't hold back. Give your call your all.

If you are not a believer yet, please consider answering the call to salvation. My experience with God and His offer to forgive me for my sins opened the door to my having a purpose in my life. I have the freedom to serve God with the talents He gave me. There is no greater joy than to have peace with God and a purpose for one's life. If you are still not sure what to do, take God at His word and trust Him with your life.

In the quietness of your own mind, pray to God like you're talking to a friend. God knows your thoughts. Simply take God at His word and trust Jesus as your Savior. Jesus died on the cross for our sins, was buried, and three days later rose from the dead—proving He has power over sin and death. He now offers eternal life if we simply believe in Him. Do that right now before you put this book down—you will be glad you did! The angels in heaven are rejoicing if you prayed that prayer—and so am I!

Credits

Most of the information dealing with Dr. Stanley Miller, the finches of Galapagos Islands, and Biosphere II came from a DVD by Lee Strobel, *The Case for a Creator*. Thank you, Mr. Strobel, for your insight and input, and for dealing with the facts.

The *World Book Encyclopedia* is responsible for the short but thorough understanding of the nine systems of the human body.

LIFE Nature Library's book titled *Evolution* by Ruth Moore and the Editors of LIFE. Copyright 1962, 1964, by Time, Inc., New York. All rights reserved. pp. 7, 10, 111-114 (noted by * in the manuscript).

Unless otherwise noted, all Scripture references are taken from the New King James Version, copyright 1982 by Thomas Nelson, Inc. Used by permission. All rights reserved.

About the Author

Mr. Palmquist comes from a little town in Pennsylvania called Townville. He graduated from high school in 1968 and went directly into the Marine Corps. While serving in the Marines, he distinguished himself by earning three meritorious promotions, several medals for special service, as well as several letters of commendation.

Upon his discharge from the Marines, Mr. Palmquist attended Florida Bible College in Hollywood, Florida. While in college, he played football, and spoke and sang at numerous youth meetings, as well as special meetings held at various churches. His artistic ability was highlighted when he designed and built two floats featured in city parades, which were held in Fort Lauderdale and Miami. He was elected student body president during his senior year of college and graduated magna cum laude in 1976.

After graduation, he moved to Indianapolis, Indiana where he worked for the 7-UP Bottling Company, and held a teaching position at Indiana Christian University. In 1988, he married his college sweetheart, Elaine Scott, and they moved to Texas to teach at a newly-opened Christian school near Houston. For the next nine years, he was the administrator of several different Christian schools in the Houston area. In 1996, he earned his master's degree from Grace College in Indiana.

And finally, he and his wife, Elaine, founded Texas Christian School in 1990 which is still currently in operation. He has been special speaker at numerous teacher conferences where he is known as a master teacher. Elaine Palmquist, his beloved wife of 42 years, passed away in 2020.

All three of their children presently work at Texas Christian School. His oldest daughter, Beckie is the executive director; his son, Jonny, coaches football and track; his youngest daughter, Debbie, is the registrar and accountant. All this brings to mind 3 John 4 which says, "I have no greater joy than to hear that my children walk in truth."